MW01234767

Sam,

It's a pleasure
that your our VP of Sales oct Comcast.
Here's something that will help you to
become even more successful in all
areas of your business & life.

Enjoy!

Prtt 2014

THE NEW RULES of SUCCESS

THE
World's Leading Experts Reveal Their

TOP SECRETS to help you achieve optimal:

- ☑ HEALTH
- ☑ WEALTH
- ☑ LIFESTYLE

Published by CelebrityPress®, Orlando, FL
A division of The Celebrity Branding Agency®

Celebrity Branding® is a registered trademark
Printed in the United States of America.

ISBN: 978-0-9886418-8-4
LCCN: 2013938202

This publication is designed to provide accurate and authoritative information with regard to the subject matter covered. It is sold with the understanding that the publisher is not engaged in rendering legal, accounting, or other professional advice. If legal advice or other expert assistance is required, the services of a competent professional should be sought. The opinions expressed by the authors in this book are not endorsed by CelebrityPress® and are the sole responsibility of the author rendering the opinion.

Most CelebrityPress® titles are available at special quantity discounts for bulk purchases for sales promotions, premiums, fundraising, and educational use. Special versions or book excerpts can also be created to fit specific needs.

For more information, please write:
CelebrityPress®
520 N. Orlando Ave, #2
Winter Park, FL 32789
or call 1.877.261.4930

Visit us online at: www.CelebrityPressPublishing.com

THE
World's Leading Experts Reveal Their

TOP SECRETS to help you achieve optimal:

- ☑ HEALTH
- ☑ WEALTH
- ☑ LIFESTYLE

CELEBRITY PRESS
Winter Park, Florida

CONTENTS

CHAPTER 1

THE MOTIVATION FALLACY, GOALS AND HUBU

By Dr. John Spencer Ellis 13

CHAPTER 2

GO BEYOND WHAT'S BEEN DONE: CREATING THE ULTIMATE CUSTOMER EXPERIENCE

By Dr. Neal Patel 23

CHAPTER 3

BE OMNIPRESENT: STAY ON TOP OF CUSTOMERS MINDS FOR A NEVER-ENDING CLIENT LIST

By AJ LeBlanc 31

CHAPTER 4

HOW TO RAISE YOUR FAMILY FOR SUCCESS

By Adam Walker 41

CHAPTER 5

YOUR DIGITAL DNA™: THE BUILDING
BLOCKS OF YOUR ONLINE SUCCESS

By Lindsay Dicks 53

CHAPTER 6

**LASTING PERSONAL AND
BUSINESS SUCCESS**

By Con Antonio 61

CHAPTER 7

LOGIC IS THE KEY TO FAILURE

By Deb Cheslow 71

CHAPTER 8

SUCCESS DOESN'T WEAR A WATCH

By Gayle E. Abbott 79

CHAPTER 9

**GRABBING ONLINE TRAFFIC FOR
PROFIT:** NEW DEVELOPMENTS

By James Datey 89

CHAPTER 10

MARKETING THROUGH STORYSELLING:
THE POWER OF REPETITION

By Nick Nanton & JW Dicks 99

CHAPTER 11

**DEVELOPING A PERSONALIZED
POA (PLAN OF ACTION)**

By Lynn Leach 109

CHAPTER 12

CHANGING BAD HABITS

By Michelle A. Bates 121

CHAPTER 13

FROM FARM BOY TO WEALTH ADVISOR —
HOW TO ACHIEVE WILD SUCCESS <u>AND</u>
SLEEP WELL AT NIGHT

By Montgomery Taylor 129

CHAPTER 14

**THE FIRST RULE OF SUCCESS
IS MANAGING STRESS!**

By Katrina Luise Everhart, RYT 139

CHAPTER 15

**THE MAGIC OF THE WORLD
AND HOW TO MAKE THE
IMPOSSIBLE POSSIBLE**

By Marcel Marvel.. 149

CHAPTER 16

ENTREPRENEURSHIP

By Patricia Hudon 163

CHAPTER 17

A REFLECTIVE LOOK AT COMMITTING TO SUCCESS

By Laura Clancy 173

CHAPTER 18

NEW RULES OF SUCCESS FOR BALANCING WORK AND FAMILY FOR WOMEN

By Sapphire Gray 183

CHAPTER 19

SUCCESS TO AND THROUGH RETIREMENT

By Ron Campbell 197

CHAPTER 20

GOT SUPERPOWERS?

By Victoria Comfort 205

CHAPTER 21

MINDSET COMES BEFORE SUCCESS

By Gregory Pierre-Louis..213

CHAPTER 22

IS YOUR GLASS HALF FULL?

By Robert Caltabiano 221

CHAPTER 23

THE NEW RULES OF SALES SUCCESS

By Preston Rahn 231

CHAPTER 24

THE NEW RULES OF MARKETING SUCCESS

By Greg Rollett 241

CHAPTER 1

THE MOTIVATION FALLACY, GOALS AND HUBU

BY DR. JOHN SPENCER ELLIS

When people think of success, they often think of personal development and motivation. Motivation is an important aspect, but it's often over-rated. Becoming motivated and inspired simply makes you feel good, but don't necessarily move you in the direction you need to go. How many times have you attended some type of inspirational or motiva-tional event? How many hours have you listened to a motivational audio program, and felt very inspired, and yet still lacking the specific direc-tion that was necessary to fulfill your dreams? My good friend Topher Morrison calls this the "happy clappy" syndrome. You get pumped full of sunshine, but you still do not have the tools, techniques, resources or specific strategies to get what you want in life.

Let's just say you have a financial goal of earning $100,000 in the next year. You attend a motivational workshop. You feel full of vigor, and feel as if you can conquer the world. It's almost as if you are bursting at the seams with anticipation of reaching this financial goal. It is a long flight on the way home from this workshop. You have time to go over all of your motivational strategies. You lay out your goals and specific plan - so you think - to reach this financial quest.

Once you get home and recover from your jet lag, you discover some-thing very, very important. All the motivation in the world has only got-ten you excited, and perhaps given you more energy than you thought was possible. But still, as you sit down to put your plan into action, you realize one very important thing. You do not actually have a plan of action. It's almost as if you're revving your engine, but staying in neutral.

Suddenly it dawns on you. You never learned any specific strategies, tactics, techniques or any specific plan to reach your financial goal. BUMMER! All you have is motivation, but no direction. So what do you do? This is the time and the place for a reality check. You need to be clear and specific. You need to ask yourself and answer honestly. What specifically do you need to do? What do you need to know to make your dreams a reality?

It is time for your reality check. Will your current business give you the income you need? Do you have a mentor or coach to help you reach your goal? Are your current expenses too high? Do you understand the technology that may be necessary to reach your goal? Do you have the proper support system in place to reach your goal?

Is it starting to become clear why motivation and inspiration just isn't enough? And yet, on the other hand, having a specific plan without motivation is not good either. Ideally what you need is the proper combination of each of these elements.

There are two opposing theories for successfully reaching your goals. One school of thought says that you need to become motivated and then find your passion and use that motivation to reach your goal. The other school of thought, the one that I subscribed to, says that you must first find your bliss and your true passion. Then the motivation comes much easier. Once on your way, I think it's good to alternate your learning and practice of both motivation and application.

Let's take a moment to discuss two important things. The first are your goals themselves. The second are your daily actions. Goals can be defined as many different things. In essence, it is what you plan to do in the future. This can be by the end of the day, by the end of the week, by the end of the month, by the end of the year, or at some point in the distant future.

Your daily actions are what you get done each 24-hour period. Plain and simple. "You only get paid for done." I've always liked that phrase. *You only get paid for done.* In short, you can make all the plans you want, but you only get paid for what is accomplished by way of your daily actions.

If you think about it, who really cares what your goals are if you never do anything each day to make them your reality? You can make your list of goals as big, crazy and lofty as you like. It may make you feel good in the moment. But, if your daily habits, rituals and actions are zero, or next to zero, none of that will ever matter.

Let's change your imaginary goal here for a moment. Let's say you want to drop 20 pounds of body fat by the end of the calendar year. If you are starting in January, or even June, this is a very reasonable goal. Now let's imagine that your daily habits and rituals are completely incongruent with your goal. Your daily ritual includes poor food choices, bad sleeping habits, and a lackluster approach to your daily exercise rituals. It is highly unlikely, if not impossible, for you to drop the 20 pounds you desire. Once again, this is because there is complete incongruency between your daily habits and rituals and the goal that you set for yourself. There must always be absolute congruency.

Let's break this down a little bit further. Your daily habits and rituals are not just focused on a particular long-term goal or many long-term goals. Your daily habits and rituals have to do with every aspect of your day. Before I go on, I need to express one thing. Obviously, there will be days where you just need a break. There will be days when you are on vacation. There will be days that you are sick. There will be days when there is a family emergency. However, aside from these days, you have to stay on track and be consistent. It is the only way you will ever reach your desired goals.

If I may, I'd like to share with you how I organize my daily habits and rituals. First and foremost, I make sure that I get adequate, deep and restoration sleep. I go to sleep at the same time and awake at the same time. To enhance the quality of my sleep, I even have a ritual before I go to bed. I am strongly recommending that you do the same. I'm not suggesting you have the exact same ritual, however, I am suggesting that you do have a ritual.

In that hour preceding sleep, I make sure that the room I am in is dark. This helps your body prepare for sleep. I never exercise right before bed. It raises the core temperature, which also inhibits quality sleep.

In addition, I will have a tea called Kava, which helps promote quality sleep. Everyone responds a bit differently to this tea, but I have found it to be incredibly beneficial. As I walk upstairs to go to sleep, I imagine myself getting more and more relaxed, and I visualize deep and restful sleep. You can think of it as playing a game, but in fact, it does work. Make sure that your bedroom is as dark as possible. This also allows for proper hormone secretion so you can have deep sleep.

My daily exercise routine is structured and yet playful. I know roughly 80% of what I will do each day of the week for my workout. However, I allow the other 20% to be interpreted during the time of my exercise. This allows me to adjust on the fly according to how I'm feeling, and how my body is responding to the day's workout.

Aside from being a success coach, I have been involved in the health and fitness industry since 1992. And I have to admit, during a good portion of this time, my eating habits were subpar. They were never horrible, but they certainly could have been better. However, now, my eating habits have improved considerably and I have a specific daily ritual to ensure I have a well-balanced and proportioned diet. The result has been nothing short of incredible. Now, in my mid 40s, I am in better health, and my sports performance is at a higher level than at any time in the past.

This is not the time or place to talk about a very detailed or specific meal plan. However, there are some general rules that you can easily live by to improve your daily rituals of improved nutrition. Eat 4 to 6 times each day. Eat smaller meals. Ensure you have a protein and as much fiber as possible at each meal. Avoid flour, sugar and salt as much as possible. If you are going to juice, make sure that you are juicing more vegetables, as opposed to fruit. This will reduce your rapidly absorbing sugar intake. I am also an advocate of nutritional supplements. Remember, a supplement means "an addition to" something, not "instead of" something. Sound nutrition always comes first. Then add supplements to fill in the gaps where your diet may be lacking. Aside from feeling better, improving any sports activities, and feeling more confident poolside, eating properly has one very important benefit to you. When you feed your body properly, you have the energy and the mental clarity to better accomplish your goals.

I also have a daily to-do list. On this list, there are the obvious things such as going to the store, or making a call, or doing some type of home-related task. Whenever possible, I delegate as many lower-level tasks as possible to people that work with me in the capacity of a contractor, employee, or virtual assistant. By doing this, it allows me to focus on my HUBU, this is the "Highest Use and Best Use" of my time. We will get to a discussion about HUBU in a little bit.

For me, my daily to-do list is a micro view of my annual goals. Each day I update my daily to-do list. Each day, it allows me to take yet another step towards the completion of my annual goals. I am strongly encouraging you to take a similar approach. Make your daily rituals, habits and to-do lists a micro-reflection of your annual goals.

Even though having daily, weekly, monthly and annual accomplishments are inspiring, to some degree it can also be exhausting. Your will power has to be developed just like a muscle. Also like a muscle; it can only last so long each day. I have learned over the years that I need to set aside some time each day to just reflect and recover. This is above and beyond my obvious nightly sleep. I have also found that having a day of rest, recovery, recuperation and reflection is also vital to staying on course, staying motivated, and maintaining sanity on the way to reaching goals.

Each day, I will set aside at least 30 minutes to do nothing other than close my eyes and relax, go for a very slow contemplative walk, meditate, do some yoga, or sit on my patio and look at the greenery. Which activity I decide to do is based on how I feel in the moment. This portion of my day is left up to interpretation at that given point in time.

You need to have this as part of your daily ritual for success. Determine what you will enjoy most. That is not to say that you can't have more than one thing that you do for mental and physical recovery. For variety, you may have three or four things that you do. Just simply ask yourself what seems to be the best choice for that day.

There is irony here. Although this time in your day is to take a break and recharge, it is also a time that can be most inspirational to you to develop your next great idea, or to gain the needed clarity on an existing goal. Think of this on a macro scale. Don't you get some of your best ideas, or become the most inspired, when you are on vacation? If needed, you can think of this short break each day as a mini-vacation.

My actual workday is broken into specific segments. For me, I prefer to be able to complete a task, or at least get a good portion done to a definitive point, if I am going to start it at all for that day. It can be a bit aggravating at times to have 10 or 20 projects that are each less than 5% completed. From a neuroscience point of view, these are called open loops. You can think of it like this. When someone has a significant event in their life, they often say, "All I want is closure." We, as humans, desire that sense of closure or completion. Having 5, 10, 15 or 20 open loops in your life can make you feel a little disjointed. A few open loops are to be expected. That is just part of life. However, having too many open loops leaves your brain fatigued, and it reduces your ability to focus on your major goals.

Take a moment to self-assess. How many open loops do you have in your life right now? If it helps, you can subdivide or categorize these open loops. How many open loops do you have in your personal relationships? How many open loops do you have in your health, fitness and wellness plan? How many open loops do you have in your annual goals list?

We can take this down to the micro level. How many open loops do you have for today's to-do list? Too many open loops can make you feel anxious, nervous, uneasy, aggravated, short tempered, or any of the other negative emotions that have to do with having unresolved issues. It is time for you to close as many loops as possible. The feeling is incredibly liberating.

One thing we have not discussed yet, but really need to at this point, is the fact that all of your goals must be congruent with your values. It is never advised to try to live someone else's life, or fulfill someone else's dreams, or define your goals to try to pacify or satisfy someone else. It is only when your goals and dreams are aligned at the highest level of your core values will you actually realize these dreams and then benefit from them completely. Stand in your truth, not someone else's.

Let me give you some examples to help illustrate this point. Let's just say that your highest value is safety. And you also have a goal of skydiving for the year. This is complete incongruency and likely will not happen. Another example would be having a goal of earning your black belt in karate – while one of your most sacred values is that you could never strike another person, regardless of the situation.

Here is another one that I find both interesting and all too common. If you have a strong belief that wealthy people are greedy, stingy and selfish, then you must understand that you will never become wealthy. It would fly in the face of your current belief system and values. Why would you ever want to become a wealthy person if you think wealthy people are this way? At a subconscious level, your brain would stop any emotion, idea or strategy that would make you wealthy. It's a matter of self-preservation at a subconscious level. It sounds strange, and it's true. If you truly believe that wealthy people are 'a-holes', why would you also have a goal to become wealthy and become one of those 'a-holes'?

My friend and cast member from my movie *The Compass*, T Harv Eker, said something that really resonated with me. He said, "Love and embrace what it is that you want, or want to become." Still today, I find this to be of great value. There is no reason to not love and embrace what it is that you want to attain, achieve or become. If at any time you have found yourself jealous or envious of someone who has more than you, i.e., money, power, influence, etc., you have likely found that this did not serve you in any way.

Right now, take a moment and think if you have any feelings like this. Is there any person, group or organization that can help you, but somehow you feel resentful or envious towards them? If so, stop it right now, unless you can tell me how being bitter, angry, envious, improves your health or gets you closer to your goals. I didn't think so.

Make a list of people or organizations that make you feel these negative emotions. Write down why you think that might be the case. Then write down why and how you will change your emotions and associations. Then, most importantly, take action and follow through. Remember to love and embrace what it is that you want to become.

Okay, now it's time to discuss your highest use and best use of your time, also known as HUBU. By now, I am sure you are familiar with the 80/20 rule. Also known as the Pareto Principle. It states that 80% of your results will come from 20% of your efforts. In business, it also states that 80% of your problems will come from 20% of your customers. From an industry-wide perspective, it states that 20% of the people in your field will do 80% of the business. It goes on and on. For the intent of this chapter, we are going to talk about the first example.

What do you do best that will give you the highest percentage of results and the greatest sense of accomplishment? Think of it like this. If there are 100 tasks needed to reach your goal, what are the top five or ten things that you can do on a daily basis that are the highest use and best use of your time so you're able to reach your goals?

Yes, I think the 80/20 rule is good. However, if you can get it to 90/10 or 95/5, that is better yet.

I am sure that you have heard about working on your weaknesses. I think that is good advice to a point. However, if you only work on your weaknesses, your strengths will weaken themselves over time. There is something else to consider as well. There may be a reason why you have a weakness. It may be because you absolutely despise doing that task. If that is the case, why would you want to spend any more time doing it if it ultimately can be automated, outsourced or eliminated? What is more important is to understand <u>what you don't know</u> and <u>acknowledge what you do not like to do</u>. Then have the common sense to hire someone to do it for you.

It seems the most challenging part about HUBU is the "letting go" process. We, as forward thinking entrepreneurial people, often feel a need to maintain total control. There is no possible way to maintain control over everything - ever.

I want you to think about this for a moment. You can only have total control when you also have the ability to let go of control. By letting go of unwanted and unneeded tasks, you have the control and the ability to understand your highest use and best use of time more so than someone who can never let go of anything.

I have found it helpful to check myself on a periodic basis throughout the day. I literally ask myself, "Is this the best use of your time and talent?" If the answer is no, I stop doing it immediately. Then, I decide if it can be eliminated, automated, or delegated. If needed, I take the necessary action and move on to something that is better use of my time. Until you get the hang of this, you may even consider setting up some type of periodic reminder that prompts you to check your HUBU status.

20

In closing, I want to remind you of something that is very important. The point of the journey is not to arrive. The point of the journey is the journey itself. It is not as if you reach a magical epiphany, a Shangri-La of sorts, and all of your life's goals and missions are complete. You will never have a magical moment where you think that you have accomplished all there is to accomplish, seen all there is to see, or felt everything there is to feel. It always has been, and always will be, a matter of levels and degrees. There is always another level to reach, and always another degree of understanding. There is always something else to experience.

Make sure you also take time to relish the small accomplishments on your way to your bigger goals. This isn't to say you get lost in the minutiae. It's as simple as periodically reminding yourself why certain things are important to you, and why you even began the journey in the first place.

About John

Each week, over one million people enjoy a fitness and personal development program created by John Spencer Ellis. His programs are used in the top resorts, spas and fitness centers. John is the CEO of the National Exercise & Sports Trainers Association (NESTA), Spencer Institute for Life Coaching, International Triathlon Coaching Association (ITCA), and the Mixed Martial Arts Conditioning Association (MMACA).

NESTA is the parent of Wexford University which offers Associate through Doctoral degrees in fitness, nutrition and sport psychology. John created Adventure Boot Camp, the largest fitness boot camp system in the world. He also created Intense Mixed Performance Accelerated Cross Training (IMPACT), Kung-fu Fitness and TACTIX. He created programs used by Cirque du Soleil, Army, Navy, Air Force, Marines and Coast Guard, and consults the UFC (Ultimate Fighting Championships).

Contact John at: http://www.johnspencerellis.com

CHAPTER 2

GO BEYOND WHAT'S BEEN DONE: CREATING THE ULTIMATE CUSTOMER EXPERIENCE

BY DR. NEAL PATEL

When I began my dental practice five years ago from scratch, I soon became well aware of one crucial fact…

…nobody wanted to come in for an appointment.

This isn't to say I had some kind of inferiority complex or my care wasn't very good. No, the truth of the matter is nobody really wants to go see ANY dentist – unless they have to.

Is that kind of mindset really the best for a doctor-patient relationship, on either side? That's why I was determined to avoid the tried and true when it came to running my dental practice. I wanted to see happy faces coming and going, as much as possible. If I was going to improve people's smiles, I may as well get to see them in action, right?

I learned the "New Rules of Success" on the way to reaching that goal. They apply to virtually any other business. So sit down in my chair for a few minutes and find out how I turned the traditional dental practice upside down. And don't be scared – I promise it won't hurt!

RETHINKING THE BUSINESS OF DENTISTRY

When I started my dental practice, I didn't have many thoughts about doing things differently. I thought I would be a "normal dentist." I'd buy a chair, get a drill, get the appropriate numbing agents, install the big light and start working on patients.

After I had my set-up in place, however, it became clear to me, as I saw patient after patient approaching our offices with trepidation, that most people were actually fearful of the whole dental experience.

Now, after you've studied dentistry the number of years I had to study it, you forget how other people might view your services. In your mind, it's about helping with whatever treatments are needed to solve an oral issue – and nothing more.

But in your *patients'* minds, there's a whole lot more going on. And I came to understand that their fear and dread was getting in the way of my providing the best possible care – because patients either would skip appointments or not make them in the first place.

The number one thing I had to understand was how dental patients felt – and put myself in their shoes (or put on their dental bibs, to be more accurate). I had to understand what they were afraid of – and try to remove or minimize as many of those phobias as possible. What was the focus of a dental patient's anxiety? Clearly, needles, pain and the discomfort of ongoing or lengthy treatments topped the list. Well, the problem is, of course, some of those will always factor into dental treatment, I couldn't completely eliminate all those negatives – but what I *could* do was design a practice that would put patients much more at ease.

That, to me, would require nothing less than a complete "rewrite" of how a conventional dental practice should operate. Instead of just assuming things should be done how they had always been done, which had been my initial approach, I had to think through every element and decide how best it served the *patient*...rather than my process.

Of course, whenever you rewrite the rules of a well-established business, you take a big risk. I had to believe in myself and my ideas to enough of an extent that I could follow through with my new ideas. My entire business plan had to change so that my efforts revolved around what was easiest for the patient, rather than operate like a traditional dentist making the traditional profit. In other words, the concept of seeing a certain number of patients a week or performing a certain number of specific procedures to ensure a certain level of profitability had 'to go out the window.'

Becoming customer-centric could have meant that I would take a loss. But I felt, if everything was done for the consumer, and, in turn, appreciated by the consumer, then everything else should fall into place. If I could create a dental practice where patients could actually feel something different taking place, something they *like*, more should want to come in for appointments.

MAKING THE BIG CHANGE

Here are the main principles I decided I wanted my practice to be based on:

- The patient's treatment should be as pain-free as possible.
- The patient's experience should be comfortable and as enjoyable as possible.
- The patient should not be afraid prior to an appointment.
- The patient should understand the treatment thoroughly and feel in control.

Let's start with that last one. You have to understand it took me four years of education to be able to properly interpret a dental X-ray. So, if I show my patients an X-ray and explain what I see going on, those patients are probably going to nod their head as if they understand – even though, in all likelihood, they don't.

That means I had to find another way, a more efficient way, of showing patients their problems and why the treatment is important – in terms *they* could understand. I've done that by adopting as much digital technology as possible. Everyone is more and more comfortable with that kind of technology, because of their smartphones and tablets – and they actually trust it even more than they might trust me or any doctor's opinion. And, because I take the time to use the tools they themselves do – and explain things in language they're comfortable with – some of the traditional walls between doctor and patient are taken down.

Why is that important? Well, in the past, dental patients have had to assume that the work the dentist does on them is necessary and appropriate. If they didn't fully understand what the dentist was doing, however, that naturally boosted their anxiety levels; by properly informing them, however, through understandable language and visuals, they don't have to assume *anything*. I open a line of communication in which they can understand their choices and literally chime in at any point. They don't just have to sit in my chair, stiffen with apprehension and wait for whatever I might decide to do to them. Instead, we're partners in the process - and they know I care about how they feel about what's going on.

Ultimately, this allows me to perform at higher levels and have more satisfaction in the service I'm providing. I don't have to worry about opinions the patient is afraid to share, because I make sure to get those opinions before they walk out the door. And I sleep much better for it.

This attitude of openness and respect for the patient is ingrained in each member of my staff as well – and it's also allowed me and my staff to feel really confident in what we do and to feel really good *about* what we do. The patients validate us through their positive feedback and give us credibility through their results. The usual dentist office, I think, is more concerned with controlling the patient than empowering the patient. Having our patients respond to us as having value, instead of just being pain-inflictors, brings a lot more clarity to our professional roles.

When you do what's best for the patient, when you do what's best for the consumer, the result is that you're rewarded in many, many different ways. Business people, far too often in my opinion, get upset because they don't feel appreciated for what they bring to their customers; they often get hung up on things that should not matter, such as the cost of technology and of providing services, and how to increase their overall profitability by delivering less.

That shouldn't be the driving force in a business – the driving force should be to make a difference in people's lives, with whatever product or service you're selling. When your focus is strictly on providing a superior customer experience, you're going to be rewarded by those customers because they see the effort that's going into taking care of them. That becomes a big win-win.

THE ULTIMATE ROI: REINVESTING IN YOURSELF

I've been lucky enough to have my rethinking of the traditional dental practice pay off, as mine grew really quickly. Of course, that leads to another interesting crossroads for a business; do you take the extra profits you make and take a great vacation or buy an expensive sports car for yourself…

…or, do you take the money and simply reinvest it in your business to make it even better? To me, the answer was simple – I put those funds back into the practice to take the patient comfort and care factor to the next level in two specific ways – by upgrading our amenities and our technology.

When it comes to amenities, we offer everything from neck pillows to blankets to their favorite coffees and other beverages. Of course, many dental offices do that – but it was just the start for us. How many other practices have a pastry chef who provides European pastries? … Or fireplaces throughout the office? …Rooms that have been converted into small libraries and dens? …Or a facial and esthetic spa for patients?

Why do we need all that? Well, because it helps anyone who has to wait for their dental treatment to be as comfortable as humanly possible. If I'm behind on a procedure or attending to an unexpected emergency, people aren't in the waiting room reading a two year-old *People* magazine. Instead, they're watching TV, surfing the Internet on Wi-Fi we provide, or enjoying a complimentary facial from the esthetician we employ.

It's also important because it shows we respect the most valuable asset our patients have these days – time. These additional services make the impact of a dental appointment less invasive to their schedule and their livelihood – we are literally offering everything they can find in the comfort of their own homes (and then some), as well as providing something in return for the time they've invested in coming to our offices.

The results have been amazing. Some patients actually stop by my practice for a cup of coffee on their way to work. And we truly welcome that. Not many people go out of their way to visit their local dentist when they don't even have an appointment!

My other major reinvestment was, as I noted, on the technology side, and towards the same end – increasing the patient's comfort. One of the big game-changers in that arena has been 3-D Imaging; it eliminates the need to cover our patient's teeth with some goopy stuff that makes them gag for two minutes just to get a model of their teeth. Instead, I actually have a camera that scans their teeth, takes the data in through CAD software and allows me to design any devices I need to create for treatment, right in front of the patient.

Not only that, but I also have a modeling machine that can actually *make* what I design in five minutes. Traditionally, if a patient needed a crown for a tooth, it required several appointments – and they would have to wear a temporary crown for several weeks before the real one would be finished. Now, we can do everything in *one* visit, and that saves us and them a lot of time.

What my practice has really become known for, however, is the 3-D X-ray, which really eliminates the guesswork. With the old school X-rays, sometimes when a patient was in pain from a tooth, the dentist couldn't be positive about which tooth was the culprit. That was not the doctor's fault, it was a limitation of that technology. Now, however, 3-D X-rays allow me to literally zoom in on a specific tooth – and see everything from the nerve inside of that tooth to a small infection that's less than the size of a BB. Because a diagnosis is now so much more precise, it means a less invasive treatment for the patient, along with less pain and a faster recovery time.

Everything I've put back into my business has honestly allowed me to subsequently *grow* my business in an exponential way that wouldn't have happened with a traditionally-run practice. Most businesses rely on marketing techniques to grow their customer base. Those are effective in their own way, but the best marketing I've seen comes from the testimonials and referrals of the people who trust and believe in what I'm doing – my patients.

Why do they believe in me? I think it's because they see that the $200,000 I might have spent buying a Rolls Royce for myself was instead reinvested into increasing the level of their comfort and care. And they know that my practice is also kind of my playground, where I do what I love to do. They can tell I take pride in our offices, because they're pristine, with no clutter, the equipment is at the absolute cutting edge of what the field has to offer and my employees have a passion for and a confidence in what we're able to offer to them.

One more important point – even with all these "extras" I've added to my practice, my fees are still quite comparable to competing practices. The traditional assumption would be that somebody has to pay for all the bells and whistles that we've acquired – and that my patients would have to pay a lot more for what they get. The truth of the matter is that, because I've integrated this technology at the highest levels, it has actually lowered my costs. Because it's mostly digital, I save on material expenses and, because it enables faster diagnoses and treatments, it cuts down on "chair time" – which means I can see and treat more patients that need my help.

Obviously, I've created a lot of "New Rules of Success" that are specific to my practice. But, again, I think the spirit of what I've done applies to any kind of business. You don't just set up, hang out a shingle and do everything the same way everybody else does – I tried that and found it didn't work for me. I believe you have to invest in your business at a level that the public can see and appreciate – even when it comes to your own development. For example, I've put a lot of energy into improving my knowledge of dentistry – to such an extent that I've become an educator who lectures around the world on dentistry and technology, so other dentists can understand what I've done and implement it in their practices. I believe most people should take the time to become a leading expert in whatever their specialty is.

The bottom line, for me, is what kind of experience are you delivering to your customers? Is it the "same-old same-old" – or are you really trying to up the ante and take your product and/or service to a level that is really going to get people excited about you and your business?

Success comes from standing out from your crowd of competitors. Satisfaction comes from out-delivering your customer expectations. Deliver a world-class experience – and you'll receive a lifetime of both.

About Dr. Neal

Dr. Neal Patel, dentist and international dental educator, is a graduate of The Ohio State University where he earned degrees in both molecular genetics and dentistry. Excelling in the arts, Dr. Patel searched for a career that would allow his artistic ability and passion for science, to shine.

While under the post-doctoral fellowship of world-renowned prosthodontist, Dr. Edwin McGlumphy, he experienced and mastered the fine details involved in using advanced technology to perform reconstructive dental surgery. Achieving that level of precision fueled his desire to deliver nearly flawless results in his own practice. Dr. Patel recognized that the patient, *his top priority,* got to reap the benefit of beautiful esthetics, less discomfort and faster healing.

In addition to his cutting-edge private practice in Powell, Ohio, he is currently on an international lecture circuit, educating the world's dental clinicians on the modern technologies available to the dental industry. Dr. Patel teaches 3D digital imaging and computer-guided surgery. He has mastered the art of maximizing the patient experience by always granting the very best of treatment, which can be done only by embracing digital technology.

To promote his passion for dentistry and devotion to the patient, Dr. Patel has designed an equally impressive state-of-the-art facility for his private practice. Every detail, from the sleek contemporary décor to thoughtful patient amenities, reflects his vision of surpassing patient satisfaction. His patients include people from all over the country, who are willing to travel to benefit from the innovative technologies he uses in every facet of patient care. And while the equipment is important, the advanced training Dr. Patel and his staff have undertaken *to use* the equipment is equally important.

He has published numerous clinical articles on advanced treatment techniques and business strategies, including *Forbes, Newsweek, Journal of the American Dental Association* (J.A.D.A), and more. He is a consultant for a number of dental manufacturers and works closely with the research and development sectors for product development and enhancement.

Dr. Patel strives to provide the ultimate in comprehensive dental care and education for all.

CHAPTER 3

BE OMNIPRESENT:
Stay On Top of Customers Minds for a Never-ending Client List

BY AJ LEBLANC

You've heard of Coke, Kleenex, Google and Xerox. Chances are, you used one of these (now generic) words in a sentence today. Why are these brands so recognizable to consumers?

Because they mastered the art of "**Constant Consideration.**" They took risks, never retreated, and created brand solidarity, making them always top of mind for their consumers. Any business owner who is serious about wanting the same esteemed status needs to learn and craft their brand in the same way.

You may be thinking to yourself, *"Why should I listen to this guy?"* I built a top-ranked, award-winning multimillion-dollar software company called Car-mercial that leads the Automotive industry in online video marketing. Not only did we disrupt the way automotive dealers did business, we pioneered 3 new video marketing software platforms, sky-rocketing us from 3 to 60+ employees in a very short period of time. A little search engine called Google actually just published their first case study on an automotive video marketing company and chose mine as the subject of the study.

I know you are busy, so I did my best to compile the best 'Omnipresent' quick tips for your own consideration, so you can get started on your own success story immediately.

OMNIPRESENCE EQUALS CONSTANT CONSIDERATION.

1. Pre-market: Engage, experience, be passionate.

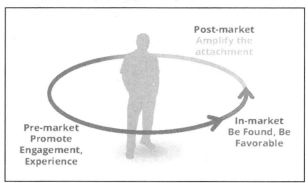

- In order to grow, focus on the trends that matter. You started your business most likely to solve a problem in the world – whether you are a B2B or B2C, do your homework first to make sure you are solving the problem in the most efficient way possible. After all, if you want to instill passion for your product in others, you must first be a believer yourself.

- Trust your instincts with keen foresight. Anticipate every obstacle imaginable and visualize how it would realistically affect your business. No need to dwell on the negative Devil Advocates; however, you do want to plan properly so you are ahead of the curve every time.

- Ignore what the competition is doing! For some reason, this seems to be the most difficult tip for new business owners to digest. Obviously you want to stay on top of industry news and trends in general, but reading too deeply into what others are doing or even worse, trying to copy their model, is unnecessary and distracts you from your main goal: delivering the best world-class product / service possible. As long as your head is in the game for the right reasons, you will find competition will start trying to copy you. Be a leader, not a follower.

- Avoid naysayers and hone your vision. As long as you have your own personal support team – whether it be friends, family or colleagues and business partners you can trust, don't listen to negative people who may have other motives for bringing you down. If you know you have a great business idea, and you have the research to prove its need, then your personal support team should be validation enough to start moving full steam ahead.

- Don't get comfortable. Building a business takes a lot more time and effort than most people realize. You can't practice the "just enough to get by" attitude, as it will only deliver you mediocre results (at best). Did Obama campaign just enough to win the Presidency? Did Michael Phelps practice just enough to win the Olympic gold medal? Did Steve Jobs make Apple products just a little bit more different that the competition's products? The answer is all these people achieved greatness in their goals because they went above and beyond average efforts to achieve the top spots in their respective fields. And even after maintaining these accomplishments, they had to keep pushing to maintain them. Did Obama get cozy in the Oval Office just because he won once, or did he campaign like crazy the second time around? Did Michael Phelps slow down after winning his umpteenth victory medal in the Olympics? No, he continued onward and won more gold medals making him the most decorated Olympian of all time. Did Steve Jobs stop after he launched the iPod? No, he launched the iPhone and the iPad, creating an entire new way humans interact with technology.

Comfort is a luxury that savvy business people cannot afford. It tends to translate to laziness, which leads to plateaus. In my opinion, an example of a great American company losing market share from not reinventing itself is Sears. Sears used to dominate the country and was the go-to place for merchandise for the American family. Sears stopped reinventing itself once it got critical mass in the market, and eventually was overtaken by companies like Walmart, Target and Home Depot. Resting on your laurels can be a bad judgment to make; historically, the economy has gone though ups and downs every 10-20 years – in every industry, so statistically your industry will have good and bad times. Not planning for what is historically inevitable is not good business and can leave you scrambling to cover operating expenses if the economy takes a turn for the worse.

• Remember that you don't need to hit a home run every time – you can hit a lot of singles and doubles that will lead to a winning business. Every small, actionable step you take brings you that much closer to Omnipresence in the marketplace.

• You will feel the pain of sacrifice – remember, if it were easy, everybody would be doing it and enjoying the sweet taste of freedom by way of extra income. Warning Disclaimer: at times, there will be 80+ hour work weeks, you will lose sleep, you will not get paid, you will lose a semblance of a social life, and you will lose precious time with loved ones. Still hungry for success? Good, then you passed the first test. Keep reading.

2. In-market: Be found, be favorable a.k.a. BE THE BEST POSSIBLE PRODUCT / SOLUTION.

• Commitment to end vision: remember that knowledge is power. For example, at the time this was written the U.S. consumer spends a yearly average of 107 hours reading versus 1,095 hours watching television (that is *10X* more time spent with eyeballs fixated on a screen). I applied the same rules to the auto industry and its potential customers – hence Car-mercial.com was born. I brought commodity to the auto industry and created more engagement with potential customers.

• Teamwork: strategic partnerships and mutually beneficial business alliances can bring an average company to new heights overnight. This is a mindset I bring with me to all my companies; specifically at Car-mercial, we brought in some of the most recognizable names in the automotive industry to strengthen our brand's credibility and extend our reach to new customers and clients.

• Problem solve – don't retreat, don't give up, don't bury your head in the sand and wait for the problem to go away…or else your competition will rightfully take your market share while you are not looking. Feedback is always an incredible tool to have in your arsenal; don't be afraid to ask for it, test its merit, then use it to fine tune and adjust your product or solution along the way.

Also, if you are tracking your results / measuring your performance, and if the numbers aren't what you had in mind, make sure you find out why before adjusting anything major. Hire a professional firm if necessary. But whatever you do, don't guess or assume anything.

- High touchpoints are crucial – be in front of potential customers at each and every point of the engagement and sales process, all the time. You can't just send a once-a-year holiday card and expect loyal fans to come knocking down your door. Touchpoints mean: e-mail, phone call(s), meetings, direct mail, events, social media, videos and more! As new technology comes out, you need to learn it and figure out how it can apply to your business model. Embrace new touchpoints – don't be afraid of them - and get creative with ways to get **Constant Consideration** from customers.

- Nobody remembers 2nd place

3. <u>Post-market</u>: Amplify the attachment.

- Measure success. Don't keep shifting side to side, or you'll never move forward.

- Set the bar as high as you can and achieve it. Next, surpass those expectations. Reset and repeat.

- Never surrender. Just like Coke and the Kleenex's of the world, narrow focus. For example, just because you sell baseball caps pretty well, doesn't mean you should also go into the sweatshirt, sweatpants, towel and lanyard business. Be a master of your niche first before expanding into additional product or service offerings.

- Don't take things personal. People will want what you have, but won't want to do what you did to get there. Get used to it. Never feel guilty for your success – you are working hard for every penny!

- Fight for your right to own your marketplace. Just because somebody was a customer once, doesn't necessarily mean they are a lifelong customer, or even a repeat customer. Try not to take any of your customers for granted by continuously communicating with them and answering any questions or needs that may arise.

- Never fear failure. As one of my favorite mentors once said, *"How do you get wisdom? By gaining experiences – the best experiences are ones where you fail and learn from. Fail as quickly and as often as possible to gain needed valuable experiences and only then will you have wisdom to grow."* If one of your ideas doesn't take off, or a marketing effort completely flops, do not dwell on it. Instead, learn from the situation and move on.

4. Pay it forward:

While this tip *should* be self-explanatory, a lot of people don't seem to fully grasp what this means – so I'll try to elaborate here.

- In business – just like in life - you want to treat others fairly. Don't forget where you came from, or ever look down on one certain group of people (or anyone, for that matter). Remember, you are not different than they are – you are just working harder with significant business-boosting goals.

- Don't take advantage of people. The benefit of an unnecessary quick buck or upsell is not worth the backlash you may get from customers sharing horror stories about your company. The world is too small and too fast for any negative publicity stemming from unhappy customer experiences. Kind of like real-life relationships, if you are ever in the wrong, be the first to admit it with full disclosure and do whatever you can to make it up to your customers.

- Keep your vendors happy. Just like satisfied customers, vendors make great walking billboard testimonials for your business, leading to more referrals and more business.

- Don't take things too personal if something goes wrong – think of the tabloids and what the media covers from one day to the next. Society forgets and moves on to the next big thing very quickly.

- Consistently step up to the plate, and treat people like you want to be treated. You will prevail. You will elevate. You will accelerate. Don't look back. After all, there is no time like the present – unless, of course, you are Omnipresent.

Best of luck!

Please don't hesitate to reach out if you have any questions on how to move forward. (Another example of carefully planned Omnipresence!)

Direct: (561) 319-3227

AJ@Car-mercial.com

About AJ

Born in Connecticut, AJ lived in the small town of Cheshire until the age of 10 years old when his parents moved the family to Vero Beach, Florida. AJ graduated from Vero Beach Senior High School in 1991 and went on to complete his MBA from National University in San Diego California. AJ is the managing partner of a leading-edge digital marketing software company. Founded in 2005, AJ pioneered video marketing with Car-mercial.com, a software platform that helps automotive manufacturers, associations, ad agencies and dealerships implement digital marketing campaigns to attract, sell and service more customers profitably.

Car-mercial.com works with hundreds of new car franchise automotive dealers in the U.S. & Canada with a client list that includes numerous Ward's Mega Top 100 dealer groups and many of the #1 new car franchise dealerships in numerous different brands. Car-mercial.com delivers proven strategies to increase traffic, sales and service business through search engine optimization, video search engine optimization, social media and online reputation management. Car-mercial.com's Broadcast+ Network has 3 unique software platforms (SEO+, Display+, & Social+) that help automotive dealers engage with online buyers using the power of sight, sound and motion.

Car-mercial.com's Proven System combines the power of television's sight, sound and motion with the power of search engines' ability to speak directly to consumers who want to buy or service a vehicle now. Car-mercial.com is the first company in the world to specialize in the optimization of online TV ads that attract more traffic for less cost than traditional advertising and paid search engine marketing. Their high-impact Car-mercials have become popular because they stand out amongst the mountains of static text results and they influence consumers in a way the written word alone cannot.

Company Awards:

- 2013 PCG NADA Spotlight Award

- 2013 Dealer Marketing Magazine- Technology Leadership Award

- 2013 AutoSuccess- Best of the Best NADA

- 2013 AutoSuccess- Top Companies to watch

- 2012 Automotive Website Awards - Most Promising Technology

- 2012 AutoSuccess- Top Companies to watch

- 2012 AutoSuccess- Best of the Best NADA

- 2011 Automotive Website Awards - Best Video Optimization Platform

- 2010 AutoSuccess - Top Companies to watch

Contributing Monthly Writer to a variety of esteemed publications, including:

- Canadian Auto Dealer Magazine

- Dealer Marketing Magazine

- AutoSuccess Magazine

AJ is also the co-author of the *Unfair Advantage Book* (released fall 2012).

AJ also speaks at a variety of industry conferences, including:

- Digital Dealer Conferences

- DMSC (Digital Marketing Strategies Conferences)

- Automotive Marketing Boot Camps

- PCG Pit Stop Digital Marketing Tours

- AutoCon Digital Marketing Conference

- First Class Educators Digital Marketing Classes

- NCM 20 Groups

- ALR (Automotive Leadership Roundtable & Awards)

- NADA (National Automotive Dealers Association)

- Dealer Blitz

- Internet Sales 20 Group

Direct: (561) 319-3227

AJ@Car-mercial.com

CHAPTER 4

HOW TO RAISE YOUR FAMILY FOR SUCCESS

BY ADAM WALKER

10 Things to consider to improve your child's chance of success in life.

"Somewhere along the line we seem to have confused COMFORT with Happiness" ~ DEAN KARNAZEZ*

We in the Western world are the lucky ones, but do we all appreciate it? This chapter is about raising children for success, however you will notice very quickly the massive influence this chapter places on YOU! You are going to control the "controllables" focusing on how YOU can make an impact and save your children (& You) from an unfulfilled life!

My aim is to help you in some way, to improve your life regardless of your current status. I'll give you my opinions and ideas. Then you choose what will work for your personal situation. If it just improves your life by even 1%, then in my mind, JOB DONE.

1 – CREATE A WORLD

It is important to realise, even though we see ourselves in the physical sense, our "energy" interaction with others, outlook and thoughts do far more to define us.

You came on this earth to create your own experience. You'll work hard

---

*Ultra marathoner of 50 in 50 states in 50 days!

to make sure your children have the best opportunity to create their own successful experience. You are their guide as to what will make them mentally and physically successful now and on into adulthood.

You have got to believe. For you and your child's desire to be successful in life there must be compatibility between your desires and your beliefs to make this a reality.

Do my beliefs match up with my desires?

YOU create your own world. If you believe the World is a "bad" place (you watch too much news), it probably is for you right now and is unlikely to change until you address your current beliefs! Already this will have impacted and nurtured some negative beliefs in your children. Without intention, you are already holding them back from their optimum chance of success!

No one is a machine! All of us have belief's that help us and beliefs that don't. Just being aware of yours will help you manipulate them so they work for and not against you. Remember the best way to cultivate your next generation of success is to be a role model!

Don't just tell them. Show them the way!

2 - PUTT FOR BIRDIE!

Fig.1

*When you looked at the pictures above, your heartbeat will have increased as you glanced at the "panic"eyes on the left.

The brains of animals and humans are designed to give priority to bad news and to recognize threats first (Fig.1). This is why people can tend to be negatively dominant, which is great for basic survival, but this can hold YOU back from success!

With all these in-built tendencies, negativity/escape tend to dominate positivity/approach. We all process bad information more thoroughly than good. Which unfortunately means bad parents and negative feedback have way more impact than good parents and positive feedback!

Research has shown that professional golfers putt more accurately for a par than for a birdie. To put another way, we try harder to avoid a loss than to achieve a gain. It is our "normal" human nature; and it comes down to Loss aversion vs. Gain attraction.

This is why "normal" is rubbish and in life YOU must putt for Birdies!

3 - IN THE (COMFORT) ZONE?

With the modern weakness for instant gratification, so many of us spend the majority of our lives tucked up nicely in the "comfort zone," avoiding potential work/pain and replacing with pleasure (addictive behavior, food, drink, drugs, internet, shopping, gambling).

When in the comfort zone, how does this affect your sense of purpose and success?

"Alas for those that never sing, but die with their music in them."
~ OLIVER WENDELL HOLMES

Our whole culture is based on the lie that it's possible to be certain about the future. Choose the right school, foods, and investments and then your family's future is guaranteed! You have to give up this illusion to develop courage and get out of your comfort zone. Now you can live in the moment, embrace YOUR painful things without the mental fear of the "dreaded future event".

4 - PREVENTION IS BETTER THAN CURE.

We are in the habit of treating problems, rather than anticipating problems and 'nipping them in the bud.' I'll anticipate some of the modern family problems you are either experiencing now or are likely to in the future: -

Potential Problems:

- Packaged "Low Fat" Foods.

- Internet, Digital TV and Gaming.

- Smartphones and Tablets.

- Acceptance of poor health.

- Ignorance? *No longer a legitimate excuse!

My Solutions:

✓ Commitment to Truth.

✓ Holistic Approach.

✓ Listen to your Body.

Too simple? I feel complex systems in isolation from real world occurrences and day-to-day life are just are not realistic for the majority of our own personal situations. This is for your child/future children, not someone else's!

This solution will also establish the weakest link affecting your individual child's successful development. This should then become your priority…

Be Proactive rather than Reactive.

5 - FUEL UP & GET GOING.

What is more important – diet or exercise?

A nutritionist would say diet and a trainer would generally say exercise. As a strength and conditioning specialist I would say that keeping your nutrition in order will be far more beneficial in life than any exercise program can be. It is possible for a child to live a minimum healthy lifestyle with no exercise. However, it is not possible for a child to live a minimum healthy life with no food and water!

For success however, both are essential to the individual. The aspect that is lacking most in your situation becomes the most important for your family.

–What you feed and offer your child will determine their health.

–What exercise they are involved in will determine their fitness.

–These combined with mental health will determine their success!

6 - K.I.S.S. FOOD

Becoming a "Fitkid" or achieving optimal health through what you eat and drink on a daily basis is simple, it's not easy to do, but it is based on some simple principles.

Keep It Simple… for your kids ☺

Most nutrition focuses on the final outcome, calories consumed against calories used.

FOOD = ENERGY CONSUMED.

MOVEMENT = ENERGY USED.

In most cases nowhere near enough focus is put into the quality…

Micronutrients

Making sure your children eat a wide variety of food from an early age not only stops them growing up fussy, but it also ensures their body's micronutrient needs are met. This is not affected by activity levels and could be the only "One size fits all" section of this chapter!

Don't Count on Me!

Should you count calories? If you're looking to be successful, these are my key issues:

- A Calorie is not just a calorie.

- All fats/proteins/carbs are not the same!

- Fructose is the villain. *Very sweet & mostly metabolized into fat.

  Success Nutrition = Not counting calories!

Hormonal Kids!

Understanding that hormones have a major role in weight loss, athletic performance, fitness, general health and success is key. Your metabolism is important in the search for health/success and how you can manipulate hormonal responses will play a part. There are some simple ways you can do it:

Eat More Often.

The traditional three meals a day is convenient, a habit and not based around what is best for your body. Your metabolism wants more, when you eat your metabolism kicks in, your body has to release hormones to deal with the digestion of proteins and fats.

MEAL – SNACK – MEAL – SNACK – MEAL – SNACK

= Success Nutrition!

Leave it too long and you are way more likely to overeat quickly when you get the chance.

Fruity Loopy!

Why do you think so many companies base the taste of their snacks on fruit? Everyone loves the taste of fruit, humans love fruit and fruit loves humans. Fruit's good for us, so tuck in and bring your family up on it. Don't give them fruit flavoured "things" give them fruit flavoured fruits!

- ✓ Fruit only breakfast.

- ✓ Fruit "Washdown"! To finish each meal.

- ✓ Fruit access! Always around and accessible.

Oooo Beeeehave!

There is no doubt that there is a strong link between diet and child behavior. Children must be given a healthy and balanced diet that enables them to develop both physically and mentally.

Nutritionally poor quality and quantity =

- More frequent/intense tantrums.

- Increased problems sleeping.

Me, You, Them and Us!

Everyone is to blame! Everyone blames everyone else! Schools blame parents, parents blame schools, food companies blame computer game companies, and on and on. Everyone is partly to blame and no one is sure whom. Take your responsibility and do what you can. Children do not choose to be unhealthy. They are victims not perpetrators.

7 - MOVE & HAVE FUN!

Fitness and exercise is full of "trends" and the latest "fad," but the consistent benefits of increased energy, health, better self-worth are lifelong and come from a natural desire to move and have fun! Children shouldn't exercise, they should PLAY and it should always be fun.☺

"Work and play are words used to describe the same thing under different conditions" ~ MARK TWAIN

We all know someone who goes to the gym for up to 2 hours; the key is what did they actually do in those 2 hours. Did they have fun? Are they mentally refreshed? Why were they there two hours? Exercise duration has less of an effect on benefits from exercise than the intensity that was used.

Play with High Hormones!

If you are looking for a great time to work out or play games, around 7 am, mid-day and 7 pm will work well with your body's hormones. Even just 15 minutes of intense movement and fun would have a massive effect on your family.

8 - WORLDS COLLIDE!

Everything comes down to your choices and the two worlds you and your children live in, the tangible and the intangible:

1. TANGIBLE – Things you can touch, see, taste and hear.–
   Your body, your house, your clothes, your food, your car, and your family.

2. INTANGIBLE – Things you cannot touch, see, hear or taste. –
   Your emotions, happiness, sadness, confidence, relationships, love, positivism, motivation.

All of these elements come in to play to move towards a truly successful and optimal life on a daily basis. Being aware of this will help to enable success and will affect your family's lifestyle.

9 - GOT ATTITUDE?

In society there are a lot of unhappy people out there and they bring their negative outlook to the table. When they bump into your child, they WILL have an impact on them in some way. You can choose to ignore their negativity (avoid if possible), and when your child starts to copy you, this will be their "norm." This is a massive celebration moment! Its sets your child on the path to being successful, able to actively make negative influences bounce off his or her negative proof amour!

"Change your attitude and your behavior will follow." ~ RYAN LEE

This advice is for adults. Your children will not have to change their attitude; help develop it positively from the start and their body will follow their mind.

When it comes to successful people, if you're thinking: but it's because they are so good at what they do. This is a backward way of thinking negatively about yourself. It's not because they are so good at what they do, it is because they BELIEVE they are that good and that always needs to come first.

It's a 24/7 barrage from the outside world, so you got to put the work in to compete. Your main aim and mission as a parent and a person is very simple. Get rid of negativity!

"Learning to ignore things is one of the great paths to inner peace"
~ ROBERT J. SAWYER

Stop watching the news! It's bad. The media does not represent the good/bad equally and it can mess up your "balance" if you let it. Be proactive and get stuff done! Think of all that extra time you'll get from not watching the news daily!

Take FULL responsibility for your life. Don't whine about it, do something about it and be the most positive person you know!

10 - RAISE YOUR SUCCESS

School will teach you English, Math, Science and a few other specific subjects, but not nearly enough emphasis is spent on how to be successful! This is where as a successful parent you step in and take up the slack!

"The only limitations for your life are the limiting beliefs in your mind" ~ MATT MORRIS

The main weapon a Successful child will have that their peers will struggle to attain is belief. This is the main separation between the two. From the upbringing you provide, they will have faith in their own abilities and no doubts that they WILL achieve their desires. It is this mindset that will single your family out for success in life.

Lets go back to the basics of what life really is, what would be a successful life for you? Without doing this, it is tough to visualise the most effective path for you and your family to reach your shared and individual goals. It is only through breaking down life into its many parts, that you can begin to see what needs to done to achieve success. When this holistic approach is taken, it is actually a very simple way of thinking and will stick with your family throughout life and serve them well.

"Out of clutter find simplicity"
~ ALBERT EINSTEIN

What is success for you? What will your children look up to you for and become inspired by? Is it measured by Money? Time? Status? It's up to you and your children; no one can define success for you.

The sad reality is that most believe that life is tough and has to be a struggle. Getting fit is tough, losing weight is tough, earning money is tough and finally I'm sure you guessed it, Success is tough! I wonder what their children's views are likely to be??

Pursue your passion! You cannot fake this. If it's passion, it's not work and it's inspiring. Trust me.

Success is the experience that counts! Learning from mistakes is overrated. You do learn from mistakes, but do you need to make mistakes in order to be successful? Hell no. Observe success. Learn from others who have done, maybe made mistakes along the way (not so many) then avoid these mistakes. I prefer to learn from success! No matter how small, you can build on them. Other people's mistakes are just that and don't make them yours. Do not expect that you need to fail to achieve, it is not an essential element of success.

CLOSING THOUGHTS...

People seem to love being 'normal,' "I want a normal life, to do normal family things, to have a normal bodyweight." You need to create your own norm. Society needs better norms, but don't wait around for them.

Your success and your family's will depend not on what you have read in this book, but on your unique talent, what you take away from this book and what you apply in your daily life. Remember most people go out there with the best intentions, many just get lost along the way.

"Actions, not excuses, bring success"
~ Adam Walker 2013

About Adam

Adam Walker is making a name for himself as a "man on a mission" and the UK's Key Speaker on Youth Conditioning, Sports Performance and Success. He fuses his knowledge of Education, Nutrition, Training and Success in a way that has not been achieved before.

He founded Sport Speed Academy in 2007, and continues this work with sports teams and individuals of all ages. Adam specialises in the development of athletic power output and speed capacity. This has included International, Olympic, Paralympic and Commonwealth medal-winning sportspeople from a variety of disciplines. Visit: www.SportSpeedAcademy.com to get fast and win more!

Adam formed the UK Youth Conditioning Association (UKYCA) in 2010 having key experts come together with a common goal. The UKYCA runs courses educating parents, teachers, trainers, coaches and students on youth conditioning. The UKYCA is the first and only organization focused purely on youth conditioning in the UK. It acts as a resource and community for passionate, dedicated individuals who are involved with the U/18 population, to enhance, discover and share best practice whatever country you are from. Visit: www.UKYCA.com to join the family.

Adam currently lectures in Sport and travels the world learning, speaking at events, and has authored his own book expanding on the chapter written here for the New Rules of Success. "FiTKiD FATKiD" is due for worldwide release in late 2013: www.Fitkidbook.com.

Adam graduated from Loughborough University. He competed internationally as an athlete for over a decade. Following a nasty Polevault accident in 2008, he bounced back two years later to represent GB in sitting volleyball. Most importantly he is a proud parent to two sons Dylan and Harrison (due at the time of writing this!) with his wife Christina just South of London, UK. Each year Adam takes on just a handful of coaching clients from all over the world to achieve their success. If you want to connect with Adam, visit: www.AdamLewisWalker.com

CHAPTER 5

YOUR DIGITAL DNA™:
THE BUILDING BLOCKS OF YOUR ONLINE SUCCESS

BY LINDSAY DICKS

"You have one identity. The days of you having a different image for your work friends or co-workers and for the other people you know are probably coming to an end pretty quickly." ~ Mark Zuckerberg

Back in the Stone Age - aka, before the Internet - your professional reputation was squarely in the hands of the people you associated with. As long as you were honest, reliable and straightforward in your business dealings, that reputation stayed spotless. And whatever you did behind closed doors rarely, if ever, spilled out into your professional world.

Fast forward to today - where, thanks to posts on social media sites and elsewhere on the Internet, you're suddenly stuck explaining things you don't want to have to explain to the people you do business with. Those things may seem relatively harmless, but those pictures of you on vacation after a few drinks will suddenly become part of the professional conversation about you.

That's why one of the BIG "New Rules of Success" is that your reputation is now at the mercy of Google, Bing and other Internet search engines. Think about it; the first thing most of us do when we hear about someone we're interested in doing business with is do a search on their name to see what we can find out. What we find out in that first page of results – and through social media sites such as LinkedIn and Facebook - is critical to how we will view them professionally.

That's why our agency has spent a lot of time - and an awful lot of money - to unlock the secrets behind all of our "Digital DNA." What we found out can boost your profile, lift your business to the next level, and make you an online superstar.

How? Read on.

BUILDING CELEBRITY EXPERTS

We specialize in building Celebrity Expert® status for our clients. While they are already experts in their field, they aren't necessarily experts in communicating that to the public at large (and, most importantly, to potential new leads). Most just don't know how to position themselves in their market with the right media for their particular message – and don't really have the time to devote to this crucial task to do it right.

Just like a great movie or book needs the proper publicity launch to make people aware of their existence, our clients need a certain kind of exposure to communicate their unique personalities, skill sets and experiences to a broader circle of other influential thought leaders and potential customers. We work at making the right connections for them at the right time - using such platforms as best-selling books, programs on network TV affiliates, and articles in such nationally-recognized periodicals as *The Wall Street Journal, Inc.* and *USA Today*.

Naturally, we promote these media placements through our clients' websites and social media services, such as Facebook, Twitter and so forth, to further boost their brands. This ensures that these prestigious appearances show up as an integral part of their online identity. Note, however, that we said *"part"* of that identity.

The fact is there are a lot of facets to anyone's online identity that we don't control in this process. There may still be a lot of other personal or even professional information that might show up that could easily conflict with the main messaging we are putting out about them.

For all that other information about yourself that either you or those you know leave behind in cyberspace, we've developed the term, "Digital DNA™." Unlike genetic DNA, this "strand" is one you actually can alter to your benefit. And it can definitely be in your best interests to do so.

GOING DEEPER INTO YOUR DIGITAL DNA™

As we said, your Digital DNA™ is comprised of every byte of information that exists about you in the online world. We're talking about your personal web sites and blog posts, Facebook, LinkedIn, YouTube, personal photos, press about you and any other Internet site where you've been mentioned or where you've posted something.

If you're like most people, you've probably Googled your name at some point and either been surprised at the information that's appeared about you - or disappointed that you haven't left more of an online mark. The good news is that both situations can be corrected, and should be.

Understanding and controlling how you are represented on the Internet is the single most important business strategy you should undertake today - because again, that's where everyone at this moment in time goes to find out who you are, what you do and whether you're the person they want to do business with. It's almost like the ultimate job interview - and one that you're not even in the room for!

It's easy to see that your Digital DNA™ contains the building blocks of your success - but it only works that way if it is properly managed and continually updated. If it isn't, your online reputation will remain a big question mark - controlled by unknown factors or, even worse, actually tarnished by other parties you may not even know.

Your offline activities now pale beside your online reputation - which is more easily accessible than ever, because most of us have the Internet at our fingertips 24/7. When people want to know about you, they'll instantly jump on their laptop, tablet or Smartphone and find out what they can. Even if someone "offline" personally vouches for you, the Internet has become our *de facto* authority and can trump that recommendation.

That's because, while our memories can fade and grow fuzzy, online info remains as clear as it was the day it was posted - which might have been two, ten or even fifteen years ago. Whatever was said about you in the past, good or bad, right or wrong, isn't going away any day soon.

Because information about you is so readily available to anyone checking you out – and since they can't easily discern whether that information is right or wrong - you *must* be constantly aware of your Digital DNA™ and be proactive in controlling what story is being projected online to prospects and customers. This is a quantum shift in how people find out about you and check you out – and, even now, most still haven't caught on to its importance.

To ignore the reality of this shift and its consequences, however, is to unnecessarily put your business and reputation at risk.

OUTCLASSING THE COMPETITION

Even if you are confident that there's nothing out there in the online world that can really hurt you, there is also an awesome opportunity to *leverage* your Digital DNA™ to your advantage, if you're willing to be proactive about it. Controlling your online reputation in order to present yourself in the best possible light to all who search for you means you'll be taking advantage of the incredible untapped potential that the Internet offers you to boost your expert status.

As we said, when people perform an online search on your name, it's like the ultimate job interview. Now, imagine going to a job interview in a t-shirt and shorts, instead of your best clothes - that would be more than a little bit crazy, right? Well, not attending to your Digital DNA™ isn't that far from that outlandish example. In every other business situation, you want to look your best…and this vital one is no different?

Odds are, your competition is already hard at work making sure they look their best online. Just as you wouldn't be the only applicant participating in a job interview process, you most certainly have other people selling what you're selling online. Therefore, your goal should be to "look" better than they do, so you have the leadership position in your field all to yourself. Whoever takes that position as the primary online expert has an obvious and undeniable advantage - and forces everyone else to play catch-up.

When you work your Digital DNA™ to the max, you put yourself in that leadership position.

CLEANING UP YOUR DIGITAL DNA™

The first move you should make to really take control of your DNA is to clean up and cement your current online identity as much as you can. There are four important steps you can take to make that happen.

1. Manage Your Brand

As you set out to tweak your online presences, first *write out who you want to be seen as* when people Google you. Keep that paper with you - and keep that personal image in mind as you participate in online activities of all kinds. Build towards that digital brand - think of it as a goal and take small steps every day to make it a reality. A great idea is to set aside a half-hour to an hour a day just to focus on your online identity. This can be done by writing blogs and doing press releases on those blogs.

When you syndicate the press release, it will be picked up by online media services and many will then be posted by the search engines. Either the press release, blog or both will then appear in a Google search about you. If you do this daily, you will be adding 365 more items to your Digital DNA™ annually, which will help drive conflicting information about you lower in the search results.

2. Create Consistency

You must make your personal page on Facebook (if you have one) as professional as possible - and make sure all your social media pages reflect the same "you." It's great to showcase family, pets and all other personal activities that show you in a positive light - you just have to make sure nothing shows up that would *conflict with or contradict the online image you want to put out there*. When you post a picture of yourself on social media, ask yourself whether you want a future employer to see this picture... because there is a good chance they will!

3. Own Your Name

You might be thinking it's more trouble than it's worth to participate in Twitter, Facebook and the like. The advantage, though, of doing that is that the more places you put your name, the more SEO power your Digital DNA™ acquires. Sometimes just a couple of "tweets" can put your name on the first page of Google results - just remember to write about things you want to be associated with!

4. Be Yourself

This might seem to contradict everything we've just discussed, but, as the old marketing motto goes, "People buy people." Working with your personality instead of against it brings more authentic results than trying to be something you're not. Obviously, you want to put some filters in place and not recount some horrific fight you might have had with your spouse the other night - but you can still utilize appropriate humor as well as share your hobbies, so people can see you're a well-rounded and interesting person.

The key to all of this is follow-through. When you stay on this effort day-in and day-out, it continues to pay off and keeps your name at the top of the online heap.

GOING TO THE NEXT LEVEL

Yes, there's a lot you can do on your own to fine tune your Digital DNA™ - but, at some point, if you're going to want to really make your online reputation pop out in a meaningful and awesome way, getting some expert help is really the best solution.

That's because getting proactive with your Digital DNA™ takes a lot of effort and time, as well as some specific skill sets that you may not have. For example, you'll want to distribute online press releases and syndicate them to high-impact sites to really trumpet your business accomplishments and media appearances. You'll also want to consider posting videos based around your area of expertise, as well as creating original content in the form of articles, blogs, webinars, and eBooks. This kind of content is important to have posted at different places other than your own personal website; that way, when your name is Googled, you'll look incredibly influential all across the Internet.

And speaking of your own website, you'll also want to make sure your website avails itself of the latest SEO techniques, so that it (and you) ranks as high as possible in search engine results.

Putting all these kinds of things in motion really helps you sparkle on the Internet. When you create and continue to update a comprehensive and compelling social media presence, as well as generate the content we just described, the more positive "buzz" builds around your name. You decrease the digital "noise" while turning up the volume (and increasing the focus) on your credentials and accomplishments.

That's important, because the more (hopefully positive) content that's connected to you, the higher you rank with search engines. That directly affects your bottom line in a way you often don't even see - because it's hard to know how much business you're losing, simply because your online "story" isn't coming across correctly. All you can know is that the result is a negative ROI.

There's one thing that science has proven over the years: *small changes can have profound effects*. Every step you take to promote yourself online in an authentic and impactful way will increase the chance that a prospect will quickly understand the unique features and benefits you alone can provide. At the same time, each informative link you provide back to your talents and services is a new pathway to greater respect and increased revenue.

Whether you know it or not, your Digital DNA™ is already out there - and is directly responsible for whether a potential customer will buy from you or not. If you don't take control of it, it can't work to its fullest extent for you. Even worse, it might even be working against you.

That's why leveraging your Digital DNA™ is one New Rule of Success you simply can't ignore; your virtual identity is way too important to succeeding in today's marketplace. When you do take action, you can create an overwhelmingly positive perception that positions you as the Celebrity Expert in your field. That ultimately results in more sales, more visibility and increased profits - and isn't that really the best inheritance you can get from your DNA?

About Lindsay

Lindsay Dicks helps her clients tell their stories in the online world. Being brought up around a family of marketers, but a product of Generation Y, Lindsay naturally gravitated to the new world of on-line marketing. Lindsay began freelance writing in 2000 and soon after launched her own PR firm that thrived by offering an in-your-face "Guaranteed PR" that was one of the first of its type in the nation.

Lindsay's new media career is centered on her philosophy that "people buy people." Her goal is to help her clients build a relationship with their prospects and customers. Once that relationship is built and they learn to trust them as the expert in their field, then they will do business with them. Lindsay also built a patent-pending process that utilizes social media marketing, content marketing and search engine optimization to create online "buzz" for her clients that helps them to convey their business and personal story. Lindsay's clientele span the entire business map and range from doctors and small business owners to Inc 500 CEOs.

Lindsay is a graduate of the University of Florida. She is the CEO of CelebritySites™, an online marketing company specializing in social media and online personal branding. Lindsay is also a multi-best-selling author including the best-selling book "*Power Principles for Success*" which she co-authored with Brian Tracy. She was also selected as one of America's PremierExperts™ and has been quoted in *Newsweek, The Wall Street Journal, USA Today, Inc Magazine* as well as featured on NBC, ABC, and CBS television affiliates speaking on social media, search engine optimization and making more money online. Lindsay was also recently brought on FOX 35 News as their Online Marketing Expert.

Lindsay, a national speaker, has shared the stage with some of the top speakers in the world such as Brian Tracy, Lee Milteer, Ron LeGrand, Arielle Ford, David Bullock, Brian Horn, Peter Shankman and many others. Lindsay was also a Producer on the Emmy-nominated film Jacob's Turn.

You can connect with Lindsay at:
Lindsay@CelebritySites.com
www.twitter.com/LindsayMDicks
www.facebook.com/LindsayDicks

CHAPTER 6

LASTING PERSONAL AND BUSINESS SUCCESS

BY CON ANTONIO

"No one remains quite what he was when he recognizes himself."
~ Thomas Mann

We live in a world that we mostly do not understand, and yet we expend our energy and time in trying to control things and situations that we can't, rather than understand ourselves, which is the only thing that we have control over.

Hi, my name is Con Antonio and my first encounter of my life purpose was when I was about 10 years old, living in a modest neighbourhood in a modest home, and within our surrounds were narrow streets where the homeless "lived." It was during one of my childhood days playing in the streets that I came upon a homeless man sitting on the side of the road. Although I had seen him many times before, this was my first awareness of him as someone who had nowhere to go, and it was at this point that I put my hand in my pocket and gave him my pocket money. His gratitude and appreciation was immediate and this gave me such joy to know that I "helped" someone else. I made it my "purpose" there and then that whenever I saw my homeless "friend" I would always give him what coins I had. And carrying this forward, I have devoted my time to help and inspire others to achieve success in their lives.

In my early years of coaching, I took the approach of coaching business owners on how to improve their business. However, I noticed that once our business coaching sessions ceased, their business would eventually return to pre-coaching status. It became evident that in order for a business to remain successful, another approach was necessary, and it was at this time that I modified my coaching program to coach the individual first – in order to create the mindset for lasting personal and business success.

Several years ago one of our clients came to us confused and uncertain as to what he needed to do to develop his business and create lasting success. We introduced our coaching program to him, and he willingly committed his time and energy into developing and "getting to know himself." This in turn benefited his business. During this time, his sales increased from $450,000 per annum to $1,800,000 within 3 years – he now hardly needs to work in the business. This success story has been repeated time and time again.

Life for most people has evolved to the point where we find ourselves stuck with few choices. Life is stressful because we find ourselves unhappy with the way we feel, doing things most of the time that we don't really want to do and not achieving the things we actually want to achieve. As individuals we tend to lose our way. There has to be a better way.

In this section you will learn the five fundamental steps to achieving "lasting personal and business success."

STEP ONE

Knowing Yourself

*"Knowing others is intelligence; knowing yourself is true wisdom.
Mastering others is strength, mastering yourself is true power."*
~ Lao-Tzu

Do you truly know who you are?
In ancient Greece at the time of the great philosophers, the words *Gnothi Seauton* were inscribed in large letters over the entrance to the Athenian Temple. This means "Know Thyself" which was considered the primary essential to all knowledge by the wise men of that time.

If we are highly self-aware, then we shall be aware of our strengths, weaknesses, likes and dislikes. We would be then choosing careers, jobs and relationships accordingly. Hence we greatly reduce the chance of us meeting with disappointment. It's a lot about making informed decisions. If we are informed about ourselves, then we make correct decisions.

Self-awareness does not happen by simply spending time thinking about yourself. You need to ask yourself the right questions to get those all-important correct answers. You need to go about this in a healthy way so that you don't end up at the other extreme – which is being obsessed with yourself.

The aim of knowing yourself is to raise your level of awareness so that you will find it easier to understand what is required of **YOU** to be successful.

Awareness is observing your thoughts and actions so that you can operate from a true choice in the present, rather than acting on the basis of programming from the past.

It is about the power to act from your "higher" self rather than to react from your fear-based, "lower" self. In this way you can be the best you can be and fulfil your destiny.

Success is a learnable skill. You can learn to succeed at anything. It doesn't matter where you are right now. It doesn't matter from where you are starting. What matters is that you are willing to learn. Becoming successful is about who you have to become, in character and mind. The fastest way to become successful and stay successful is to work on developing "you!" The idea is to grow yourself into a "successful" person.

Your outer world is merely a reflection of your inner world. You are the root; your results are the fruits.

"If you don't go within - you will go without."
If you develop the mindset of a successful person, you will naturally be successful in anything and everything you do. You will gain the power of absolute choice. You will gain the inner power and ability to choose any job, business or investment opportunities and know you'll be a success. This is the essence of our Personal Success Coaching program.

Successful people understand the formula for success is **BE, DO,**

HAVE. Unsuccessful people believe the formula to success is HAVE, DO, BE. They believe "If I Have a lot of money, then I could Do what I want and I'd Be a success." Successful people understand, "If I **Become** a successful person, I will be able to **Do** what I need to do to **Have** what I want."

I believe that it is our responsibility to grow and develop to our fullest potential, to create abundance and success in our lives. For in doing so, we will be able to help others and add to the world in a positive way.

Finally, we highly recommend you consider hiring a personal coach that will help you to keep on track in doing what you've said you want to do.

We at HID Personal Success Coaching will train and help you to dramatically enhance your life. We believe that a good coach will always ask more of you than you will ask of yourself. Otherwise, why do you need a coach? Our goal is to train you, inspire you, encourage you and have you observe, in full awareness, what is holding you back. In other words, to do whatever it takes to move you to the next level in your life. If we have to, we will strip you and then build you back together in a way that works. We will do whatever it takes to make you happier and more successful than you ever thought possible.

Remember, if you want to succeed in the real world, it's going to be your positive actions that count.

STEP TWO

<u>Be the best in your chosen field.</u>

"The best is the enemy of good." ~ Voltaire

- Ever wonder how you can be the best person you can possibly be?

- Do you expect nothing but the best from yourself?

- Do you have what it takes to be the Best?

Be the best you can be.

This starts with the understanding that we are all unique in what we are going to be good at and in what we enjoy. And for that reason, it's important to find what it is you enjoy and to work excruciatingly hard at making your potential realized. Life's too short to spend it doing something you don't love.

Identifying, acknowledging, and honouring our life's passion is perhaps the most important action a successful person can take. Successful people take the time to understand what they're here to do and then they pursue that with passion and enthusiasm.

This can only be achieved through going above and beyond to break free from the general levels of mediocrity, and doing whatever it takes to reach your goals. This is a task that's much easier said than done, but it's truly the only way to achieve lasting success.

Remember that nothing happens in life and business until someone takes ACTION. So what's your passion? What are your goals and dreams? If you absolutely knew you couldn't fail.

STEP THREE

Act with urgency, courage and conviction.

"Dreaming is life in a dress rehearsal - taking Action is living"
~ Con Antonio

The majority of people today act as if life is a dress rehearsal; that is, they act without a sense of **urgency**. This is not how successful people experience and live their lives. None of us are going to live to 150 years old.

You have to ignite that part of you that can move you to substantial productivity and action.

Many great men and women have accomplished more in a short period of time than the majority of people do in their entire lifetimes, why? They have a strong enough sense of urgency and therefore act with urgency, courage and conviction. They are doing little things every day consistently and persistently, getting the job done in a safe, organized and timely manner by prioritizing, using initiative and available resources effectively.

It is amazing how much complacency businesses or individuals can have, even in uncertain economic times or when businesses are facing all kinds of risks, from competition, new technologies and changes to government legislation. Also, success could make a business or individuals most vulnerable to complacency. It seems so illogical, but it happens very easily, and it's of course deadly. Urgency is not a natural tendency, it has to be ignited and re-ignited over a period of time.

Ask yourself, if I was going to act from a sense of **urgency**, what two actions would I take today?

Write them down and then DO IT.

Go on, what are you waiting for?

STEP FOUR

Build lasting relationships

"No road is long with good company." ~ Turkish Proverb

The way we build customer and personal relationships has changed significantly over the last decade. As a result, the connection that consumers have with brands, products, and services has become increasingly complex and dynamic.

There is a reason why building business relationships are considered very important today. The reason for this is that we live in a world where the customer is 'king' and valuing him should be of great importance. On the other hand, you need to know how to build business relationships with your competitors too.

For relationships to be lasting, we must create "Goodwill" that we consider as an asset in our respective businesses. This goodwill is achieved mainly through business relationships and the reputation you carry as a business and as a businessperson too. There are many ways that can be used to build lasting relationships. However, in this chapter we will consider the five most effective ways.

1. Networking
Networking is the best way to build business relationships that last. Proper and efficient networking does not only help you gain valuable contacts but also helps in expanding your business. References can take you places and every businessperson knows this. In years gone by,

social networking was done at parties and functions. Today, the social networking websites have taken us a step further with both wider reach and wider approach.

2. Be accessible

Another way of increasing your business relationships effectively is to be accessible and easily reachable. Being easily reachable will help you gain the faith and trust of other businesses and clients. Someone who is not available at most times will lose many business opportunities. Remember that the world never waits for you. It moves on, every single second. If you can be easy to reach, it will also mean that customers don't have to go out of their way to get in touch with you.

3. Visibility

Visibility is another way of increasing your business relationships. If you are not visible in the market, you will be missed. You will lose out on a large portion of business that is available. Indirectly, you will also lose out on the references and the networking. Networking and marketing will help you in increasing your visibility. The importance of communication is not understood until you see the benefits you can gain from it.

4. Show You Care

Keep birthday records of all your clients and their anniversaries too. Send them a card every year as a token of appreciation, and if possible offer them a discount on those important days. Many leading brands and stores follow this policy. You will partially retain customer loyalty and also give customers a feeling that they are valued. Make sure that your staff is well-trained in customer operations and dealing with grievances. Also make sure you always show concern towards employees, clients and customers.

5. Solve Problems Immediately

This is perhaps the most important point while learning how to build business relationships. Business relationships are to be maintained not only with other business owners but also with clients and customers. Making your customer care operations effective and fast will help you gain the trust of clients. Clients who are not heard out with their complaints will stop using your products and services – and this will be a double loss. Solving problems and grievances on time will give you the reputation of a business that is efficient.

STEP FIVE

Anticipate needs

"The most important thing in communication is to hear what isn't being said." ~ Peter F. Drucker

Anticipating others needs is an invaluable part of personal and business growth. Any business that takes the time to act in advance to fulfil customer needs can create very loyal and raving customers.

We all want to know that we are valued by the business we are dealing with. Customers are the lifeblood of any business and should always be treated as such. Train your service staff to give complete attention to a customer.

So how can you anticipate your customers' needs?

(i). Know your customer
If you have regular customers ask questions and actively listen to what they saying. If you do not have regular customers, you could survey a target group to identify certain needs.

(ii). Observe body language
Learning how to read body language may provide you with clues as to the attitude or state of mind of your customers – placing you in a better position to more easily understand or anticipate their needs.

(iii). Be helpful
If you have a customer asking you for something out of the ordinary, act with enthusiasm in helping them. By acting with urgency your customers could be willing to discuss other important issues.

(iv). Know your products/services
Having good knowledge of your products and/or services will assist you to determine how and when you promote or offer them to your customers.

So the question is, what are you doing today to anticipate your clients' needs?

About Con

Con Antonio is the CEO of HID Group, a trusted business leader and coach.

HID Group is also dedicated to reviving the small and medium business community by providing business coaching to business owners. Con uses his 30 years of expertise in accounting and business knowledge to create efficient systems which create profit but also works in-depth with the personal development of the business owners. Con realized years ago in working with various companies, from the medical industry to the car industry, that for a business to have lasting success it is not simply about changing systems, it's about changing the mindset and habits of the business owners running the company.

He graduated from Victoria University with honours in Tax Law and Organizational Behaviour and prior to completing his accounting degree, at the age of 19 he was granted a Tax Agent's licence and that provided him with the opportunity to prepare tax returns for individuals and small businesses - that was Con's first taste of business and the self-satisfaction of helping individuals and businesses to manage their tax affairs.

After several years working for small companies he joined AMCOR Pty Ltd, one of the largest packaging companies in Australia and overseas. For the following 13 years, Con dedicated most of his waking hours to learning and developing his knowledge. He was promoted to different levels of management, working together with some of the most disciplined and toughest professionals of the group, who taught him all he knows today about business and the discipline and commitment that is required to become successful.

Although Con enjoyed achieving success in the accounting profession, he also knew that his passion was to inspire and empower people to achieve their personal and business dreams. So, at the height of his career, he decided to resign and went on to join the HID Group. For the past 13 years he has successfully coached a number of small and medium-sized businesses that, over a period of time, have more than tripled their bottom line.

To learn more about Con Antonio please visit: www.hidgroup.com.au

7

CHAPTER 7

LOGIC IS THE KEY TO FAILURE

BY DEB CHESLOW

The very fact that you are reading this book right now leads me to the conclusion that you have some big aspirations and goals for your life and that you are taking steps to make them happen. Congratulations! But, let me ask you a question: Are you being very careful to do all of those things you've been taught – all of those things you've been conditioned to do since birth in order to play it safe and protect yourself. Things like:

- *Weigh the pros and the cons...*

- *Be reasonable...*

- *Be logical...*

- *Have a Plan B...*

- *Play it safe – don't take too big a risk...*

- *Cultivate multiple options...*

- *Have a backup plan...*

If so, then let's be very clear that you are absolutely guaranteed to fail. That's right – FAIL! You are guaranteed to stay stuck right where you are because here's the cold, hard truth: Logic is the key to failure; if you want to win big in life, playing it safe, using logic and having a Plan B

71

are guaranteed to leave you coming up short of your goals – each and every time! Think about it for a moment, "logic" is nothing more than the accumulation of your current knowledge and your past experience. If you have an idea or a goal that is beyond anything you have ever done before, then how on earth can you use logic to achieve it? The answer is YOU CAN'T! And here's why: When you start pursuing something that is outside your experience, your logic is going to kick up feelings of fear, worry and doubt, which causes extreme discomfort. And, because you have been conditioned to use logic and rationality to make your decisions, it feels very natural and "right" to step back from the pursuit of your goal – this unknown thing - and retreat to the safety and comfort of your known experiences. Successfully getting past your own logic and conditioning requires **courage** – you are going to need help in order to develop a willingness and a desire to put logic aside, step outside your comfort zone, face your fears and take massive, bold action that yields HUGE results! In fact, you have to be completely illogical and unreasonable in the pursuit of your goal.

Growing up, I was encouraged to set very high standards for myself and was allowed the freedom to explore my interests and develop my talents, and was NEVER encouraged to have a Plan B, to be cautious, to protect myself or to avoid risk. As a result, I relentlessly pursued my passions in life and never allowed people or circumstances to sway me. The phrase "failure is not an option" is used as a cliché by many people; however, it truly was the motto I lived by growing up. I never even considered what might happen if I failed at something, and I never entertained the possibility of quitting anything. Because I wasn't afraid to set my standards high and based my goals on what I WANTED in life, as opposed to what I thought I could get, I made many decisions that appeared completely illogical on their face. For example, as I was entering college, I set my sights on becoming a pilot in the United States Air Force despite the fact that I was living in an era when women were not allowed to fly in combat, and that there had never been a female Air Force pilot from Virginia Tech – despite its rich, 100+ year military history. It wasn't a logical or even a reasonable goal, but that didn't matter to me. I paved new ground and defied logic every single step of the way. I even accepted a scholarship during my freshman year in college to be an Air Force engineer; a career track that would have had me sitting behind a desk designing some part of a bomb assembly or the like, but I KNEW in my heart that it would lead me down the path to becoming a pilot – and through an incredibly unlikely series of events, it did just that!

Now, that doesn't mean that the path to what I wanted was always easy or that I always got what I wanted exactly when I wanted it, but I set my goals (my standards) incredibly high, and then unconsciously put systems in place that required me to be incredibly self-disciplined – and that invoked a level of accountability that I had to live up to. I had stumbled upon the very keys to success: standards, discipline, accountability and systems.

I have always craved discipline and structure and I seem to innately systemize everything, and those characteristics were honed to a razor-sharp edge both in the Virginia Tech Corps of Cadets and in the Air Force; however, once I left the military and started working in industry, I was dumbfounded! How did the U.S. economy continue to prosper when corporate America operated so haphazardly?

Military units function efficiently and purposefully – they know what the mission is, and they get the job done quickly and effectively. Every person in the unit knows what their function is and what they are expected to do to move the unit closer to the mission objective. Of course, that doesn't mean that things always turn out exactly right, but there is purposeful action every step of the way. On the other hand, the private sector tends to move so slowly, with so much bureaucracy and so many layers of authority, it's a wonder anything gets done! As a product of Air Force training, it was only natural that, as I started my own company, I would fall back on that experience. From Day 1, I relied on standards, discipline and accountability to direct my operations and then glued it all together with systems to ensure consistent results. I was excited by how productive our operations were and how quickly we met our objectives.

It has been my privilege to get a behind-the-scenes look at numerous corporate and organizational operations, large and small, and I have concluded that one of the main reasons why most new businesses fail within the first five years and why so many companies and organizations struggle is because they have lost sight of the four main pillars of success:

- Standards
- Discipline
- Accountability, and
- Systems

Companies and individuals alike also seem to have forgotten that they – and only they – are responsible for their results. Blaming outside forces for, complaining about, and justifying lackluster results are neon signs pointing to the fact that you are not taking responsibility for your results. Until you do, your four pillars will be built on sand and will never provide the support you need to build your dreams. However, once you take full responsibility for your results and employ the proper strategies, tactics and tools to build upon this four-pillar foundation, you can create whatever level of success you choose for your business and for your life.

I. STANDARDS

Setting high standards is absolutely essential to success – be it in your personal life, on your team, in your organization or in your business. In your personal life you will only achieve as high as you reach. If you set high standards for yourself, you will achieve at a high level. If you are content to just get by, well then, don't expect much out of life. Likewise, it amazes me what some businesses will accept in terms of performance from their employees – the salesperson who makes two sales calls per month because all he does is paperwork, the sales manager who will promise anything to get a sale even if he knows he can't deliver on his promises, the secretary who is on personal phone calls or instant messaging on Facebook all day, the production worker who spends more time in the break room than on the production line, the cashier who grumbles and complains to every customer, the rude customer service associate who treats every client as a burden. It's not enough to have a warm body occupying a chair! If an employee is not adding value to your organization, you are flushing money down a toilet every single day that they are on the payroll. Worse yet, it is not at all uncommon for these substandard employees to drag down the morale and the productivity of the entire organization.

Without standards for performance, how do you sort the "eagles" from the "turkeys?" You can't be sure who is sub-standard if you haven't actually set the standards to begin with. The military is genius when it comes to standards – if you don't cut the mustard you are done! In any organization you are only as strong as the people who are working for you; you have to be willing and able to weed out the bad and recognize the good. You are never going to get where you want to go by looking the other way.

II. DISCIPLINE

Discipline is centered around following commands. At its most basic level it is giving yourself a command and then following it, come what may. It's not enough to wish for things or hope that circumstances will turn out the way you want. You have to decide what you want, commit to the decision and then have the discipline to do whatever it takes to follow through. It has been my experience that almost everyone has goals of one kind or another for their life, but they succumb to the discomfort and fear that inevitably arises when they pursue something beyond their current experience and logic gets in the way. In the business arena, I believe that most company management teams do a fair job of deciding what they want – they set objectives for various metrics within the organization – sales goals, profitability goals, safety goals, quality goals, etc. – and they do a decent job of committing to them and articulating the goals to the rest of the company employees. Where they fall short is in instilling the discipline – both in themselves and their employees – to meet those objectives come what may.

Discipline takes courage – it is not comfortable or easy to do whatever it takes. Let's face it, you can preach the party line at your employees all day long, but just like children, they are going to do what you do – not what you say. So you can't expect your staff to be disciplined if you, as their leader, are not. Think about the qualities that you most need in your employees in order to meet your objectives and then get real with yourself, do a personal inventory and see if you possess those same qualities.

Your results don't lie. If you are not getting the results you want, it is simply because you are not acting in ways that are consistent with those results. Make no mistake, discipline is a habit and it can be cultivated just as surely as you can develop the habit of brushing your teeth.

III. ACCOUNTABILITY

Accountability is so important to individual and business success that I have devoted an entire chapter to it in my book, *Remarkable Courage – A Systemized Strategy for Success*. In a nutshell, accountability is the concept of being answerable or responsible to someone for some particular action. You can be the most disciplined person in the world, but if there is no accountability, it is easy to wander off course. It is the rare individual indeed who can successfully get past his own logic and hold himself accountable day in and day out. Most people need some manner of outside accountability for it to be meaningful and motivating. When you are accountable to another person and you have to share your progress with that person regularly, something shifts inside – it 'lights a fire under you.' The idea of not performing or of letting the person down to whom you are accountable, becomes intolerable.

In the business world, many companies use some form of accountability, but unfortunately, they often use it in the wrong way – rather than using it as a means of motivating people to higher levels of achievement than they ever thought possible, they use accountability as a stick to force people to do certain things. This will never work long term; force negates everything. Accountability is an incredibly powerful tool; use it properly to light a creative fire that will burn out of control and propel you forward at lightning speed.

IV. SYSTEMS

Systems are amazing tools for your life and your business. Essentially, they are "scripts" for how certain things need to be done. The military makes great use of systems – pretty much everything anyone does in any branch of the military has a protocol associated with it. Successful companies are the same way; there are policies and procedures that detail how certain things are to be executed.

Systems can have a profound effect on your personal and professional life. I use systems and tools all the time in my everyday life and I urge you to do the same. Many of the tools I use each day are laid out in the pages of *Remarkable Courage – A Systemized Strategy for Success* – including imagineering, daily commitment sheets and accountability agreements, just to name a few. My personal systems give me a daily roadmap to follow so I stay on the path to my goals and avoid getting sidetracked by logic.

When I started my business, I drew upon my military experience and took the advice of a mentor who suggested that I run my business from Day #1 as if I already had thousands of clients. This was incredibly powerful business advice, and I am so grateful that I listened to it because the systems I put in place early on and have continued to develop over the years have allowed the company to grow efficiently and effectively.

Of course, this is where standards, discipline, and accountability come into play. Systems are only effective when they are implemented and followed! If you, your employees, or your team don't follow the systems then there is little or no consistency – that leads to shoddy product, poor customer service, and ultimately big trouble for your business or organization.

Standards, discipline, accountability, and systems are an incredibly powerful recipe for success. They are the keys to putting logic aside and having the courage to face your fears. It's all about strategy. It's all about tools. It's all about integrating these four pillars of success into the foundation of everything you do. Unfortunately, you see, it's not enough to just KNOW this information. There is a whole science behind implementation. Everyone knows things they need to be doing to achieve the results they want in their business or in their personal life, but they don't do them. Worse yet, people know that doing certain things will give them the exact opposite of the result they desire, and yet they do them anyway.

It is one thing to possess information, but changing behavior so that you – and your employees or team members – actually implement that knowledge is something else entirely. Once you understand and internalize the process of bridging this "information-action gap," you can go on to create whatever results you want – and that's where the real magic occurs. Learn the entire systemized strategy for success in the pages of *Remarkable Courage*, available at: www.debcheslow.com and other online retailers.

Have the courage to put logic aside, face your fears and step boldly into your future and your success. Think about it: Where would your life be if every time you said, ***"I Should…"*** you actually ***DID***?

About Deb

Deb Cheslow is a two-time best-selling author, speaker, corporate trainer, and peak performance strategist who has spent her entire life defying the odds to achieve goals that should not have been possible from any logical viewpoint. She is regularly sought out by the media for her perspective on achieving breakaway success in business and in life. Deb has been seen on NBC, ABC, CBS and FOX affiliates, as well as in *Newsweek, Reuters, The Boston Globe, The Miami Herald, Yahoo Finance* and MarketWatch.com, among many others.

Famous for her no-nonsense, results-oriented style, Deb is known for asking the question, "Where would your life be if every time you said 'I Should…,' you actually DID?" She shares a systemized strategy for achieving success beyond your wildest dreams that is based upon four foundational pillars – standards, discipline, accountability and systems. Deb teaches a process for looking fear in the eye and then acting in spite of that fear. She has lived a remarkably courageous life and now views it as her mission to share the strategies she has used (and continues to use) to create incredible success in her own personal and professional life with individuals, teams, organizations and companies so they can do the same.

To learn more about Deb Cheslow, her transformational programs and services, and receive her Special Report "The Success System: 4 Foundational Pillars for Breakaway Success," visit: www.debcheslow.com or call (386) 308-2155.

www.DebCheslow.com

CHAPTER 8

SUCCESS DOESN'T WEAR A WATCH

BY GAYLE E. ABBOTT

You have this driving ambition and you know you want to succeed. You may be clear on what you want and are meant to do, or you may know you want to succeed but not be at all clear on the path. Either way, if you are truly committed and take action to move along the path, you can achieve the success you desire.

This chapter may be different from your expectations, but I'm going to encourage you to read it carefully and consider its implications, because after years of study and personal experiences I've learned there are some very interesting keys to success that may not be included in the standard success literature.

It's easy to get so caught up in the idea of achieving success that we don't necessarily think objectively about what it means to us and for us personally. More importantly, if we're not careful, when events arise where we don't achieve that predefined definition of success, we may miss the very opportunity that can take us to the pinnacle of the success of which we have dreamed. Why? — We reject it. We take the path that everyone else says we need to take, despite what we "know" within ourselves to be our path. We just give up. We engage in destructive behaviors like blaming others when things go wrong, denying what has occurred, defending our actions or wallowing in emotion. Sometimes we'll beat ourselves up for our "failure," not realizing that it may really be an opportunity in disguise. Or, we may push so hard that we get in our own way.

Our studies of successful people have confirmed that each one of us has a different definition of success, a different path to achieving the success that is meant to be ours, and a different timeline for achieving success. More importantly, one person may have success in one area while another may have multiple successes in different areas.

We have met and worked with individuals who are successful in their 20's and 30's as well as those who achieve success in their 50's, 60's or even 70's. We've also worked with those who've had real success, but it wasn't enough, so they took "shortcuts" or got greedy and then totally crashed only to have to start over again.

Success is a journey and there can be different levels of success – different summits we reach before moving to the next summit. And sometimes, only when looking back with the perspective that time gives, can we see that we have had many successes and that each one was a step on the path to the next level of success. It's a tricky balance between continuing to have the drive and the ambition to move to higher and higher levels of success, and taking the time to recognize and appreciate the successes we are having in the moment. It's so easy to get caught up in societal or someone else's definition of success that we're diverted from our own path to success.

Some of you may have a very clear inner picture of what your personal success is meant to look like. Others may not be as clear and will just need to take action as opportunities become available – knowing (and I say that meaning an inner "soul" knowing) that whatever your success is meant to look like it will become apparent as time progresses. The challenge is to avoid moving into the natural human tendency of comparing yourself to others and their timeline. Remember, success doesn't wear a watch and there isn't one path to success.

All that being said, when we look at individuals who are successful, we see common characteristics. Focusing on mastering these ingredients ensures you will be on the path to success. These key ingredients to achieving success have been used time and again by very successful individuals at all levels – including CEO's, entrepreneurs and others, as well as by myself as I've progressed along my success journey.

KEY SUCCESS INGREDIENTS:

1. *Make a conscious decision to succeed.* Even if you don't know what it looks like or how it will come about, find your drive and desire. This will head you down the path and keep you motivated to do whatever you need to do including the tough, the trivial or the boring stuff. It will allow you to see options and give you the inner strength to keep moving and doing – even when faced with challenges and obstacles.

2. *Show up and take Action.* Without action nothing can happen. That doesn't mean take action without any thought, but doing something will always enable you to make more progress than just sitting around thinking about "it." Yes, you may make some mistakes, but you'll also learn and gain insights to do things differently next time. If you don't take action you're guaranteed to fail and never succeed. Taking action may take you out of your comfort zone, but not taking action guarantees you stay where you are.

3. *Don't get caught up in someone else's journey – it may not be yours.* We hear all these people selling the "KEY" to riches and success. Yet, interestingly enough, if that's not what you're meant to do, you probably won't have the success you expected. It will either be the result of you not really being engaged in the right way, or the result of the universe (and yes I know this sounds "woowoo") causing things to happen that keep you from having the riches or 'wins' that others promised.

4. *Become Self-Aware.* Objectively get to know yourself and listen to what you learn. True self-awareness, on many levels, can truly speed up your journey and put you on the fast track. It is one of the most critical ingredients to achieving success. Yes, you can make progress without it but at some point you will be limited in the success you can achieve. Become fully and objectively aware of the following factors. Who are you really? How are you perceived by others? What are your unique strengths and how can you leverage them? What is your purpose — yours to do in this life? What are your opportunities for growth and development? What is your success "roadblock"

and what can you consciously do to keep it from being activated? What practical actions can you take to go to the next level?

You'll find self-awareness is an ongoing process along your success journey. Opportunities to gain greater insight will continue to appear. There will be bits and pieces of insight that you might not be ready for at first, but that will strike you when the time is right. Successful people I've spoken with have talked about how critical self-awareness was for them on their journey. For me, it was life changing. There are a number of ways you can gain self-awareness from feedback from others to objective assessments. I personally have a bias towards making sure objective assessments are part of the self-awareness process. While I'd received feedback from managers and others along my journey, some was helpful and some was damaging or useless. When just relying on feedback from others you have to become an expert at discerning not only if you are truly hearing all the brutal truth, but also the impact of any filtering the other person is doing because of their own views and biases.

Our firm, for example, works with individuals using a suite of five highly-validated professional assessments (TriMetrix® HD and TTI Emotional Quotient) that even from the most jaded get rave feedback on the practical value of the insights. For those who really want to fast track their life and career, we combine those insights with information from the esoteric sciences. This helps individuals who are open and ready to get greater clarity on their purpose and "blueprint." As I moved along my path I found that information I rejected early on was information that was causing me to unknowingly get in my own way. Opening myself to uncomfortable insights and information from "unusual" sources, some of which were "different" from a logical perspective, had a huge impact and enabled me to make quantum leaps forward.

5. *Actively develop the so-called soft skills.* Being the best in your technical specialty may get you in the door, but it won't move you to the top of the ladder, whether in an organization or as an

entrepreneur. Learn what "soft skills" are critical for success on the path you choose. Some, like problem solving and decision-making, will be necessary in many environments. Others like collaboration / team work will be more important in some types of organizations than others. Others like leadership or management will be more important in some jobs than others. The soft skills that are needed will also be influenced by where an organization falls on the "growth curve."

6. *Learn to sell and become proficient in marketing.* So many people cringe at the thought of selling. Talk about ingrained negative beliefs. However, no matter what you do or where you do it, knowing how to sell yourself, your ideas, and the products or services of the organization you're working for will enable you to stand out. Yes, you have to have substance behind it and you have to deliver, but if you can't sell, you'll always be limited in the success you'll have.

7. *Take full responsibility for yourself, your actions and the choices you make.* Recognize that you have choices and make decisions every day. Each decision moves you along a path. Some enhance the journey and enable you to move quickly while others result in dead ends. It's easy to blame all sorts of external forces — the economy, your boss, your company and the list goes on — but people have achieved success in even the worst of times. I've seen people who, for whatever reasons, have made the choice not to hear or act on feedback they have received only to find themselves dropped from consideration for a major promotion for which they'd been a serious, if not THE only, contender. I've also seen people who know they're miserable and not motivated be so afraid of leaving the security of their current paycheck that they sabotage themselves – staying in a job that doesn't use their strengths and sapping their energy. If they're lucky, they eventually get fired, but if not they stay in the realm of misery and mediocrity – never achieving the success they're capable of having. Do something, anything and use it as a springboard for your future successes.

8. *Add Value.* No matter what job you hold, always look at how you can contribute, add value and meet or exceed the needs of

your boss and the organization. My first job wasn't even one I wanted, but I took it because the economy was awful. I decided despite everything that I had to do the best I possibly could because I didn't want to fail. I was even thrown into a project using a capacity, speaking, which I was petrified of and had managed to avoid like the plague. I did what I needed to do to meet the requests of my boss and make him look good. Not only did I eventually get some really interesting assignments, but little did I know those experiences would be the beginning of moving me toward my life purpose of speaking, facilitating and working with organizations and individuals to take them to new levels of performance and success.

9. *Always keep learning and growing.* Constant reading and learning across industries and professions helps you to go to a higher level because you have a more strategic perspective. It also helps because you can leverage ideas from one industry to enhance another. This can help you be an innovator and strategic thinker who stands out from the masses. Attend seminars, conferences and training classes especially those that are different from the subject matter you're comfortable with. Actively participate in masterminds and discussion groups with others who are driven to go to the next level. Work with a "coach" but make sure it's the right one for you and your purpose at the time. More importantly, don't sit back and wait for someone else to pay the costs for you to learn and grow -- do it on your time with your funds if that's what it takes. After all it's your life and success we're talking about. I learned early on, and have also observed that some of the most successful people are constantly involved in activities where they can learn, grow and gain different perspectives. The key is to recognize we all have different things to learn at different times.

10. *Balance knowing when to take control and when to let go.* Learn to use discernment as to when you need to be responsible and in charge and take action, and when you need to let go and listen and "go with the universal flow" that was meant for you. Sometimes you have to let go of the process and your defined outcomes to accomplish your real objective.

I had one situation where I'd been referred into a company in another state. I ran complementary assessments and, on my own nickel, travelled to meet with them for several hours of substantive discussions only to have them tell me they wanted someone with more expertise in their industry. I did something at the time that was unusual for me – I connected them with another professional in my field. I let it go and surprisingly enough several months later they called and said they were moving forward with my firm.

11. *See obstacles, challenges and difficult people in your life as opportunities to grow, learn and go to new levels.* Changing the lens and seeing problems as opportunities in disguise gives you an edge. Most people we talk with admit that it's been the tough times and the challenges in their jobs and life that have been the catalyst that allowed them to see new opportunities which subsequently moved them to new levels of success. Every challenge or tough time I've faced, and believe me I've had a few, has ultimately resulted in my stepping out of my comfort zone and getting to an even better place. For example, when I worked for a "bad boss" who I never felt I could please (but whom others loved), it forced me to eventually leave. That eventually led me down the path toward founding and leading what is now Strategic Alignment Partners, Inc. Over 20 years later I can't imagine any other path that would be as fulfilling for me personally. If you find yourself in a job or working for a manager you don't like, learn what you're there to learn and then take action to get out. Be careful not to "jump ship" too quickly because if you don't learn what you're meant to from being there you'll just keep running into similar and more difficult situations until you do learn. The challenge and opportunity always lies in reminding yourself in the middle of things that "everything happens for a reason" even though you may not understand it in the moment. Figure out what it is for you. Then "go with the flow", take action (even baby steps), and when the time is right you'll move to the next phase of your journey.

Look back over the above list and select the top two areas that are most uncomfortable for you personally. These will generally be the ones you have a knee-jerk reaction against or feel are the most difficult and distasteful, or that you "dismiss" the most quickly. Those are probably the best places for you to personally start because that's probably where your greatest growth can come.

You have true greatness within you! Don't let your comfort zone keep you from achieving your full potential. Find it, embrace it, and while you can and should learn from others, don't get so caught up in someone else's objective or definition of success that you lose sight of yours. Celebrate and acknowledge all the incremental successes you are having along the way, and know that each step you take will move you closer towards your goal, even those times when you "feel" you're stepping backwards. Success is a journey. It's your journey and no one else's. Enjoy it!

About Gayle

Gayle Abbott, President and CEO, Strategic Alignment Partners, Inc. and Mind Soul Academy works with boards of directors, executives, leaders, high potentials and teams to fulfill more of their potential and facilitate their achieving their strategic initiatives and practical performance results. She is passionate about helping people and organizations move to new levels on their journey. In doing this, she uses her sixth sense, practical business techniques and tools, the esoteric sciences and her expertise in people, communication, critical thinking, practical results and business strategy and execution to help move individuals and organizations to the next level of performance.

Gayle is an entrepreneur and leader who has run a successful company for over 20 years. She has recently been quoted in several articles in *CBS MoneyWatch*, Business newsdaily.com and *CEO Update*. She has been published in the magazine: *Dollars and Sense*. She has co-authored several books and has a book coming out in the summer of 2013. Ms. Abbott has delivered speeches on such topics as: "Increase Your Profitability and Leverage Your Time: Keys to Grow Your Business", "Achieving Your Summit: Strategies for Personal and Career Success", "Strategic Alignment for Increased Productivity and ROI", "Selecting and Retaining Top Performing Talent in a Competitive Market", "Using Competencies to Develop and Get Better Results through People", "It's Not What You Know but What You Do" and "Increasing Your Leadership Effectiveness."

Ms. Abbott has served as an adjunct faculty member at Marymount University and American University. She has her BA from American University and her MBA from Loyola College. She has won several awards for outstanding leadership over the years and has been listed in Who's Who in America, Who's Who in the South and Southwest, Who's Who in Finance and Industry and Who's Who in American Women. She is certified as a Growth Curve Strategist and is TriMetrix® HD and Emotional Quotient certified. She was recently featured as a leading expert on America's Premier Experts Show. On her journey she has experienced extensive personal growth and achieved her successes to this point by seeing the opportunities and overcoming a variety of life challenges – such as the bad manager, divorce, being widowed unexpectedly, and financial challenges, to name a few. She has learned that while we are continually learning and growing, that if we leverage our gifts and get on the right path for ourselves, there's no end to the possibilities of what we can do and contribute.

A few of her other passions include spending time with her daughter and their two Huskies, travel, reading, visiting museums, and being outdoors – whether by water, woods or mountains.

CHAPTER 9

GRABBING ONLINE TRAFFIC FOR PROFIT:
NEW DEVELOPMENTS

BY JAMES DATEY

It is just another Monday morning; or so Patricia thinks. Hands firmly holding the wheel of her mid-sized Toyota Camry sedan, she suddenly turns right on Main Street to avoid a minor fender-bender. She is running late and a lot has happened since she got out of bed at 6:15 this morning.

Immediately after the radio alarm dragged her from her slumber, she checked her smart phone for any urgent business to handle. She brushed her teeth and took a quick shower. Lucky for Patricia, Jim her husband loved to cook so breakfast was already waiting for her. She kissed him good morning and sat down to eat but not before opening her laptop, checking the news and opening her Facebook page. She loved these mornings when everything seemed calm and ran like clockwork before the morning rush began. She didn't know what sparked the sense of déjà-vu she experienced when she glimpsed the ad for the weight loss program. It showed the typically dramatic before and after photos. Pulled from her reverie by the tantalizing smell of the waffles on her plate she told Jim how delicious they were. The local radio station played Elton John's, "Don't Let the Sun Go Down on Me"; the perfect soundtrack. By the time breakfast was over she consulted her Smartphone a couple of times and sent a few e-mails. It was all part of her morning routine almost identical to the nightly routine she followed – sending a couple of e-mails and checking out a few social networking sites before going to bed at 11.

An hour later and she is still caught up in morning traffic so she checks her phone and though it barely registers, there is that weight loss ad again. It is now highly unlikely that she will make it to work on time. Unfortunately, Patricia will probably need to stay late or bring work home with her – meaning more time connected to her laptop and less connecting to her husband.

As she is turning left on Second Street, Patricia suddenly realizes what caused that sense of déjà-vu earlier when she had seen the ad. The weight loss advertising banner on her Facebook page had struck a chord because she has been seeing it everywhere online for the last few days; on her computer at work; on her laptop at home, and even on her Smartphone. She wonders why she has never heard about this program before if it is so popular.

Patricia is still unaware that she has been retargeted.

Does this seem familiar to you? Have you ever had the impression of noticing an advertisement banner more often than usual?

Or perhaps you have been exposed to the same advertisement multiple times without being fully aware of it. Welcome to the 21st century. You have been retargeted. This is the new realm of online traffic.

Retargeting is one of the new tools within the arsenal at the disposal of the savvy Internet marketer. Retargeting or "Audience Targeting" allows the savvy Internet marketer to track all users that have visited a specific webpage (or any online destination), and find those users across almost any site on the web. The savvy internet marketer then builds a retargeting list or "audience" of users who had visited that website, creating a powerful customized campaign tailored to those specific users and which will only be seen by those users.

Retargeting is simply accomplished tracking users who have been exposed to a predetermined site. The most common types of tracking technology are cookies; codes that web servers use to put information on a user's browser and then retrieve that information at a later time for various uses. Ad servers use cookies to set unique IDs so they can identify the same user across multiple touchpoints. When an ad server receives an ad display request from a user who does not have an existing cookie, the ad server assigns a new unique ID. On each subsequent request, the cookie returns the same unique ID, thus allowing the ad server to know that it is the same user.

THE NEW APPROACH TO TRAFFIC

Retargeting remains the invisible glue, that ties together all pieces of the modern approach to traffic generation. In this new approach, the different channels of communication are considered not separately, but as a continuum along a string. This continuum moves from face-to-face communication to online communication (blogs, e-mails, forums etc...) and offline communication. The specific traffic types, from free traffic (website SEO ranking, blogging, forum activities etc...) to paid traffic (e-mail solo ads, pay per click, banner ads, etc.), are organized to target each element of that continuum.

THE CONCEPT BEHIND THE MODEL

The cornerstone of this approach is to view the potential customer as an information asset that assists the Internet marketer in his market decision processes. Furthermore trust is built through multiple interaction with the potential customer.

(a) - The Psychology of Trust

Psychological research has found that information functions as a pillar of trust in online marketing. People are willing to pass judgment, with or without good information. Where examples of one's competence or reputation are lacking, people will construct whole profiles from what little information is available. Thus online trust is built by frequently providing information to site visitors. Trust is the primary element in an online customer's decision to buy. By increasing trust, the genuine marketer thrives to positively position his product and drive his potential client to the offer page when he is ready to buy.

(b) - Knowledge development:

All of the marketing touchpoints to which a user was exposed can be strung together to create an "engagement stack" – a chronologically ordered list of all the marketing touchpoints experienced by an individual user. This allows the marketer to know that the same person who saw a Time magazine display ad yesterday also arrived on a website by way of a search click today, and then subsequently made a purchase. This structure allows the edge organizations to collect tons of data on its potential client base. It knows its potential client behaviour. How much profit will be made, when investing $100 in offline traffic (ad in a newspaper asking people to go on a website) or how much sales revenue will be generated online and vice versa, are the types of questions the data analysis will provide answers to.

With this acute knowledge of its client-base generated through the analysis of behavioural data and trust built through multiple lines to convey information of communication, the edge organisation maintains it indefinitely.

TEN STEPS TO IMPLEMENT THE STRATEGY:

How can a business or individual marketer implement this strategy and drive "tons" of targeted traffic to his product with minor resources? The answer relies on **creating one's own mix of media coupled with retargeting**. So you are asking, "What's in it for me? I'm only an affiliate marketer." The answer is simple. The knowledge of traffic detailed here gives you the winning advantage over your competitors and pulls tons of money into your bank account. Whether you are already an affiliate marketer or not, this is how you implement the system.

1. **Choose a product to promote online.**
   If you are a vendor, you probably have your product already. If you are an affiliate marketer, there is a great deal of networks offering products to promote. For beginners, clickbank (http:// www.clickbank.com/marketplace.htm) is a good way to go. There are also other affiliate networks such as: PayDotCom and e-junkie and more. For greater returns, the products you choose need to satisfy some basic requirements. The product must be popular (Clickbank provides an index of products' popularity). Their sale page must provide clear and meaningful information to a potential client and their offer needs to be compelling.

2. **Think of a catchy topic relevant to your audience.**
   There are hundreds of tools that can help you find interesting topics for your audience. You can first go to: http://www.adwords.google. com/o/KeywordTool where you can retrieve many keywords related to your product. You can go to Amazon: (http://amazon.

com/gp/bestsellers/books/) and search for bestseller books on your product. Those books have sold thousands of copies. People have bought them because they address their concerns. Finding a topic from here is highly recommended because issues discussed in these books have already proven to be of interest to your targeted niche. You can also search on: http://www.dummies.com for links with your keyword. The Dummies collection is published by Wiley Publishing. A great deal of research is conducted before books in the collection are written and published. Issues that are driving your audience's attention at the moment are probably in those sources.

3. Write an article on a catchy topic.

When writing an article, there are three main things you should keep in mind:

(a). The title of your article should not only inform the reader about its content but also attract your audience's attention. Without an enticing or sexy title that will attract the reader's attention, your article will not be read. A great technique that works for me is to include the keyword you are tackling along with the benefits associated to it that will be covered in your article. The keyword will help optimize the chances of your article being found by search tools. The benefits are obvious to the reader. This is a winning combination.

(b). The body of your article must provide real content to the reader. Do not write a long text. Your goal is to hold your reader's attention from the introduction to the conclusion.

(c). Your conclusion is a call to action. You want the reader to click on the link you provide in your article, which goes either to your product offer page, or capture page. Driving your reader to your capture page allows you to gather his coordinates and market to him over and over. This is my preferred option because if managed properly, you have your subscriber for life. Even if you are not interested in writing an article, there are thousands of tools that can help you craft one. You can make use of PLR (Private Label Rights). Here, you can access ready-made articles that you can modify to your own needs. You want people to begin to recognize your brand and become familiar with your work, so taking a few minutes to tweak and update the content will help to develop articles that are exclusively yours. Examples or good sources of PLR are: http://www.plrassassin.com; http://www.idplr.com; http://7usd.com. The first is one of my preferred. You can even use a ghostwriter if you're still feeling doubtful about your writing skills. You can find one on: http://www.fiverr.com or www.odesk.com. Fiverr is a site where people will do thousands of things for five dollars. You'll be amazed what you could find there.

4. Submit the article to EzineArticles.com and a link back to your site.

There are hundreds of ezines where you can be published: ezinearticles.com; ArticlesBase.com; goarticles.com; articlecity.com; searchwarp.com; are few examples. What you need to consider before making your choice is their popularity and standing. The right one will continue driving you quality traffic even years after your articles are published. My favourite is: ezinearticles.com. They even offer online training to refresh your writing skills which is what I suggest you do in order to fast track your future articles to publication.

5. Copy the article into your blog and post on your site to add content.

The blog is a great way to get traffic because you can use a variety of different methods to promote it. If you create useful content, people will start linking to your blog. You'll start receiving visitors from other trusted websites. You can use: http://www.wordpress.org for your blog. You'll find a plethora of WordPress training online.

6. Create a short video, demonstrating what you wrote about in your article.

Video is a cost-effective marketing platform. You must use web videos as part of your content to reach out to potential customers. A well-executed video can effectively build solid relationships with your site visitors. There are many tools that can help you create a great video. My preferred tool is: Kodak Play touch, which is inexpensive, and records in full HD. You can also use:

camtasia to record directly from your computer. If you want to edit you can use either: Adobe PremierPro (Win) or FinalCutPro (Mac). Consuming a video is effortless to your audience and allows you to get your message across easily and effectively.

7. Post the video and include a link back to your site in the description.

With video websites it's never been easier to use the power of viral video to generate fresh traffic to your websites. All you need to do is develop a video or slideshow presentation that highlights your giveaway and directs people to your squeeze page. Moreover, you can, from a single location (TubeMogul.com & Pixel-Pipe.com,) blast your video to over a hundred video publishing sites. Include in your video your website or offer page URL to drive tons of traffic back to them.

8. Post your article and the video on your Facebook page and drive more traffic.

Post your video or display links to your video on all your social media platforms including your main site and blog; Facebook and Google+ page, tweet it and include them in your LinkedIn profiles.

9. Use key elements of your article to develop solo swipes and banners and run paid traffic.

PPC (Pay-Per-Click) advertising is about bidding for the top or leading position on search engine results and listings. You do this by buying or bidding on keyword phrases that are relevant to your products or services. The higher the bid, the higher the spot on the search results, the more people who will find the ad (and click on it) to go to your website. You then pay the bidding price each time a visitor clicks through to the website.

With solo ads, a list owner sends your e-mail to his subscribers. This allows them to click on the link you provide with your e-mail which then directs them either to your offer page or your website. The advantage of paid traffic is that it is available in an almost unlimited quantity and you do not need to be concerned with SEO and changes to Google's search algorithm.

10. Retarget, retarget and retarget.

Retargeting, as mentioned earlier, will allow you to follow anyone who has once visited your product page or web page. Your marketing material can be displayed to them whenever they have their browser opened. You can decide which banners you want to display to them and how many times you want them displayed each day. Success is almost guaranteed using this targeting strategy. The visitor was on your site, hence, was probably interested in your product. You can therefore offer him similar products in the same niche or products that are complementary to your offer. There are many companies that provide retargeting services: http://www.sitescout.com is my favourite.

Your data analysis: Retargeting allows you not only to use your traffic highway to reach your site visitor when you want to, but you can also collect behaviour information of your site visitors. This can be analyzed in combination or separately to further develop a complete knowledge of your audience behaviour. For instance, you will know how much potential profit you make in sales of product X by investing in retargeting. You could even know how much profit you make in online sales by investing in offline advertisement.

Still doubting your abilities? No problem. Another viable option is outsourcing your project to experienced freelancers. You can easily find a trustworthy professional from the following freelance marketplaces: http://www.odesk.com/; http://www.freelancer.com; http://www.Guru.com; http://www.Scriptlance.com). Odesk is my favorite.

CONCLUSION:

The 21st century has arrived with the rise of Smart phones and tablets. To most technophiles, this is a revolution similar to the birth of radio or television. This technology has significantly altered the relationships that people maintain with their friends, their families, their communities, their work and even their relationship with the technology itself. These changes have had a major impact on traffic generation as I have highlighted here.

If you are a seasoned Internet marketer, a novice marketer, retired or an employee willing to generate a good income per month extra, you can easily implement the outlined strategy, make use of the new instruments, remain on top of the traffic and conversion game, and be in profit online.

About James

James Datey is the founder and CEO of Gettec Media Corp. Gettec Media is active in the development of Internet solutions for businesses and particularly in the area of traffic generation. James is above all, a seasoned internet marketer; he specialized in traffic generation and conversion methods. His approach to traffic generation combines the development of multiple sources of traffic organized to target the different channels of communication with potential clients and a maximum usage of new tools as outlined in this article.

To learn more about James' traffic generation system, please visit his website at: www.jamesdatey.com. Newsletter subscribers will receive two special reports and one e-book covering different aspects of traffic generation and conversion methods.

www.jamesdatey.com

CHAPTER 10

MARKETING THROUGH STORYSELLING:
THE POWER OF REPETITION

BY NICK NANTON & JW DICKS

Chemist Dr. Bill Mitchell thought he had created a winner back in 1957 – a sugary powdered orange drink that was vitamin-enhanced; kids would love to drink it and parents would love to buy it for them, since it had marketable health benefits. His employer, General Foods, agreed with him.

In 1959, the product finally hit the store shelves – but, despite it being advertised as having more Vitamin C than orange juice, it did not find itself making its way to many American breakfast tables. Families just weren't ready to drink a powder-based beverage in place of real juice.

General Foods had a problem on its hands.

Fortunately for the corporation, NASA, the U.S. space agency, had a problem too. The astronauts on its fledging flights complained about the bitter taste of the water supply, which was a byproduct of the space capsule's environmental system. When the agency didn't come up with a solution, one astronaut simply brought along a packet of Bill Mitchell's creation along for the ride and poured it into the vehicle's water. Flavor problem solved.

And so it was that millions of people watched astronaut John Glenn eat applesauce and drink Tang, the name of Bill Mitchell's brainchild, as he became the first man in the world to orbit the earth in February of 1962.

General Foods knew a marketing opportunity when they saw it. And soon, space footage was making its way into Tang commercials, which heavily emphasized the fact that this was the beverage *NASA had specifically chosen* for its astronauts to drink on their missions – giving it the appearance of having the approval of the scientific community, even though John Glenn's choice was just a fluke.

Sales blasted off. And, thanks to some clever marketing, so did the perception that Tang, was in fact, *created by* NASA for the space program, giving it even more scientific credibility; it quickly acquired the aura of a cool, futuristic "beverage of tomorrow." Today, Tang brings in a billion dollars a year in revenue – only the twelfth brand in Kraft Foods' history (the company bought General Foods in 1990) to do so.

And that billion-dollar brand only came to life because of some brilliant StorySelling.

StorySelling is an awesome marketing strategy in which entrepreneurs, professionals and businesses craft a compelling narrative that helps them hold on to their existing customers – as well as draw in new leads. Our new StorySelling book will explain in detail why stories are so powerful – and how to create a narrative that does the job (and more) for you. In this chapter, however, we'd like to talk about how properly marketing your story is most definitely a New Rule of Success!

PROPELLING YOUR STORYSELLING MARKETING INTO OUTER SPACE

It's clear from Tang's exemplary example how StorySelling can make marketing infinitely more powerful, memorable and impactful. In the sixties, the space race was the coolest undertaking America was involved in; baby boomers like Tom Hanks, who went on to star in *Apollo 13* and produce the HBO mini-series, *From the Earth to the Moon*, grew up obsessed with it. By attaching itself to NASA's efforts, Tang became as cutting-edge and amazing as a man walking on the moon.

Of course, the problem with this particular StorySelling direction was that, as the space program began to wind down, so did Tang's popularity (luckily, declining sales in the U.S. have been offset by (for some unknown reason) skyrocketing sales in Asian markets).

That's why, to build lasting value with no expiration date, the StorySelling marketing of a Celebrity Brand should be more evergreen in nature. This marketing strategy can also be utilized to play off of current trends and fashions if need be, rather than just being about those trends and fashions.

In this chapter, we're going to look at how to StorySell your values creatively and consistently through all aspects of your marketing. And we're going to do that by using as an example a guy who's as good as anybody at doing just that – even though he certainly lacks the futuristic luster of the Tang/NASA combo.

We're talking about Dan Kennedy, the legendary direct marketer, who has built a thriving multi-million dollar business empire through the StorySelling process we just described above. In 2012, we were excited to collaborate with Dan the Man on a best-selling book entitled, *Marketing Miracles* – and we can all learn a lot from his example.

With that in mind, let's take a look at some of "Do's and Don'ts" that we've seen Dan apply to his own StorySelling marketing over the years – and that you can apply to yours.

1. *Do* Apply Your Core Values to Your Marketing

Dan has successfully positioned himself as something of a "throw-back," a traditional marketer who shows disdain for today's slick advertising – and who, instead, gives his devotees the "No B.S." truth on marketing. He has taken his old-school approach so far as to imply that he doesn't even use email or the internet – he does all his electronic communication by fax! Dan's "herd," as he calls them, loves his eccentricities – as a matter of fact, they help bond his followers closer to his brand, as they feel they "know" Dan on a special level that outsiders don't.

If your StorySelling narrative is powerful enough, you should be able to follow Dan's example and use your values and personality consistently in your marketing to attract more and more into your own "herd." You'll build more of a *personal* relationship that takes you beyond simple business-customer transactions to something more lasting and powerful.

2. *Don't* Speak the Wrong Language

Dan Kennedy uses plain language to communicate in his marketing, because he knows he's mostly talking to conservative guys who are looking for a shortcut to success (although he definitely has a lot of women practicing what he preaches as well). You, in turn, should make sure you're talking in the right way to your audience.

Are your clients more educated and sophisticated? Or do they need to be led by the hand with a simpler approach? Do you need to sound young and innovative? Or older and experienced? Language is critical in your marketing to connect with the right potential leads – so make sure you strike the right tone.

3. *Do* Play the "Name Game"

Think about finding a catchy way to nail your narrative by giving yourself a new nickname you can place prominently in your marketing? For example, Dan K. calls himself "The Millionaire Maker." We all see countless examples of this every day – for instance, an IRS attorney who might call himself "The Tax Expert" or a dentist who bills herself as the "Smile Specialist." These nicknames are, many times, easier for people to remember than your real name – just make sure you can lock up the Internet domain name before you settle on one!

4. *Don't* Over (or Under) Sell

Dan K's audience *expects* to get the hard sell from him – they don't mind his continual marketing because that's what he's all about (and, more importantly, they also want to learn from and emulate what he's doing).

A business like a legal practice, of course, is a whole different story – potential clients don't want to feel like they're getting hustled (and the profession also has many rules in place that govern how attorneys can market themselves). That means a hard sell approach can be hard to pull off.

Your specific sales approach can range from merely providing potential customers with legitimate and useful content all the way to an over-the-top "Crazy Eddie" style of screaming sales pitch. You have to determine what works best for your specific

StorySelling narrative – and what your typical client or customer is expecting from you.

5. *Do* Make Sure Your StorySelling Has the Right "Look"

The visual element of marketing often makes a much bigger impact than any words you're using. Think of Nike's spare use of its "Swoosh" logo – or Apple's consistently elegant advertising design; in both cases, the brands' visual StorySelling registers almost immediately with the viewer, meaning they never have to waste time explaining who they are.

Similarly, Dan Kennedy is famous for his "low-tech" approach to his marketing visuals – encasing an information kit in brown paper bagging would not only be accepted but applauded by Kennedy-ites. They don't expect elegance – as a matter of fact, that's something to be distrusted in Kennedy StorySelling. "No B.S." means no frills when it comes to design (although even Dan the Man has updated his online look in recent months, presumably to continue to attract younger followers).

6. *Don't* Ignore Any Opportunity to Market Your Narrative

Dan Kennedy's attitude pervades everything he does: Whether it's a simple email or a complete book, his narrative is always firmly in place – and is always selling his Celebrity Brand on some level.

Your StorySelling narrative should be suggesting to you an overall attitude that comes through in every marketing move you make, from your LinkedIn profile page to your YouTube videos to your website copy. Check out Dan Kennedy's stuff – and you'll see a clear and consistent tone throughout…which brings us to our final "Don't"…

7. *Don't* Violate Your Narrative!

Actor Bill Murray is now known for doing a variety of dramatic movie roles – some of which have gotten him Oscar nominations. However, in 1984, he was mostly known as the goofball lead of such hugely popular lowbrow comedies as *Ghostbusters* and *Stripes*. So, when the actor played the lead in a serious version of W. Somerset Maugham's philosophical novel, *The Razor's Edge*, audiences (and, mind you, they weren't large audiences) were confused – and Murray's attempt to alter his StorySelling narrative backfired badly at the time.

Similarly, if Dan K came out with an academic dissertation on marketing, announced he had received his PhD and requested that everyone call him "Dr. Kennedy," many of his followers would be completely thrown for a loop – unless it was some kind of elaborate joke (which, knowing Dan, it very well could be!).

Once your audience is accustomed to seeing you a certain way, they are inclined to reject any radical attempt to present you in a different way. That's why you have to be careful in terms of being consistent in your marketing approach.

By the way, this isn't to say you can't change your narrative as you evolve – it's actually smart if you do. But you have to take baby steps. Murray eventually changed his StorySelling image by taking *supporting* dramatic roles that had elements of comedy in them. These were movies that weren't necessarily aimed at Murray's fans - and brought him in a whole new audience that would accept him not playing the fool.

The above Do's and Don'ts give you a rough guideline for how to successfully implement your StorySelling into your marketing materials. But there's one last all-important step to take in order to make your StorySelling really stick...

THE POWER OF REPETITION: IT'S A WONDERFUL DEVICE

We all know what happens when a snowball rolls downhill; it continues gathering more and more snow until it grows and grows in mass and force.

That's exactly what happens to your Celebrity Brand when you apply StorySelling to all aspects of your marketing. When we say all aspects, we mean all aspects - we're talking about:

- Business cards
- Websites
- Newsletters
- Billboards
- Direct mail campaigns

- Letterhead
- Email signatures
- TV ads
- Radio ads
- Brochures
- Promotional items
- Social Media
- Internet marketing
- Online videos
- Magazine Ads
- Holiday Cards
- Logos and Design Elements

...and whatever other marketing efforts you're planning or already have in place. The idea is to plant the seed of your narrative – even if it's just a slogan – wherever you can.

The association between NASA and Tang, which we discussed at the beginning of this chapter, couldn't have happened with one single advertisement – it had to be done through *relentless repetition*. An old marketing axiom has it that, at the point when you're finally completely sick and tired of your own message, that's just about the time that the public is just *beginning* to pay attention to it. You deal with your marketing constantly, so it's very easy for you to overdose on your own message. However, your public is a different story, and your message is only one of thousands they going to be exposed to on an everyday basis.

That's why you need to create a *cumulative impact* through repetition to really stand out with your StorySelling marketing.

If you don't think repetition has power, consider the case of the Christmas movie classic, *It's a Wonderful Life*. As of this writing, this almost seventy-year-old black and white film is shown yearly on NBC around the holidays; no other film like it gets that kind of first class treatment. Not only that, but many popular TV series continue to reference and spoof its well-known plot – so most of us are probably of the opinion that this movie has *always* been well-known and beloved.

However, in 1974, It's a Wonderful Life was a not-so-wonderful flop that was virtually forgotten; even the owners of the rights to the film didn't think it was worth anything. They failed to renew its copyright that year and the movie entered the public domain.

That meant any TV station in the country could show the movie *without having to pay for it.*

And they did – every Christmas. Every first, second and third-rate TV channel would repeat the movie endlessly, simply because they could sell advertising for a couple of hours that cost them nothing to program. Only *then* did *It's A Wonderful Life* – and it's unique narrative – finally become a part of our holiday rituals, so much so that a production company found a way to reclaim the copyright, resulting in NBC paying big bucks to an exclusive long-term deal to license the movie for annual showings.

If your narrative works for your StorySelling purposes, then it needs to be a part of ALL your marketing – even when you think it might be overkill. Sticking to a consistent storyline – and finding new and fun ways to tell your tale – is a powerful method of reminding your "herd" of who you are and why they like you...especially in today's crowded marketplace.

About Nick

An Emmy-winning director and producer, Nick Nanton, Esq., is known as the top agent to celebrity experts around the world for his role in developing and marketing business and professional experts through personal branding, media, marketing and PR to help them gain credibility and recognition for their accomplishments. Nick is recognized as the nation's leading expert on personal branding as *Fast Company* magazine's expert blogger on the subject and lectures regularly on the topic at major universities around the world. His book *Celebrity Branding You®* has also been used as the textbook on personal branding for university students.

The CEO of The Dicks + Nanton Celebrity Branding Agency, an international agency with more than 1000 clients in 26 countries, Nick is an award-winning director, producer and songwriter who has worked on everything from large-scale events to television shows with Bill Cosby, President George H.W. Bush, Brian Tracy, Michael Gerber and many more.

Nick is recognized as one of the top thought leaders in the business world and has co-authored 16 best-selling books alongside Brian Tracy, Jack Canfield (creator of the "Chicken Soup for the Soul" series), Dan Kennedy, Robert Allen, Dr. Ivan Misner (founder of BNI), Jay Conrad Levinson (author of the "Guerilla Marketing" series), Leigh Steinberg and many others, including the breakthrough hit *Celebrity Branding You!*

Nick has led the marketing and PR campaigns that have driven more than 600 authors to best-seller status. Nick has been seen in *USA Today, The Wall Street Journal, Newsweek, Inc., The New York Times, Entrepreneur Magazine* and FastCompany.com and has appeared on ABC, NBC, CBS, and FOX television affiliates around the country, as well as on FOX News, CNN, CNBC and MSNBC, speaking on subjects ranging from branding, marketing and law to "American Idol."

Nick is a member of the Florida Bar and holds a J.D. from the University of Florida Levin College of Law, as well as a B.S./B.A. in Finance from the University of Florida's Warrington College of Business Administration. Nick is a voting member of The National Academy of Recording Arts & Sciences (NARAS, home to the Grammys), a member of The National Academy of Television Arts & Sciences (home to the Emmy Awards), co-founder of the National Academy of Best-Selling Authors®, and an 11-time Telly Award winner. He spends his spare time working with Young Life and Downtown Credo Orlando and rooting for the Florida Gators with his wife Kristina and their three children, Brock, Bowen and Addison.

About JW

JW Dicks, Esq. is America's foremost authority on using personal branding for business development. He has created some of the most successful brand and marketing campaigns for business and professional clients to make them the credible celebrity experts in their field and build multi-million dollar businesses using their recognized status.

JW Dicks has started, bought, built, and sold a large number of businesses over his 39-year career and developed a loyal international following as a business attorney, author, speaker, consultant, and business experts' coach. He not only practices what he preaches by using his strategies to build his own businesses, he also applies those same concepts to help clients grow their business or professional practice the ways he does.

JW has been extensively quoted in such national media as *USA Today, The Wall Street Journal, Newsweek, Inc.*, Forbes.com, CNBC.com, and *Fortune Small Business*. His television appearances include ABC, NBC, CBS and FOX affiliate stations around the country. He is the resident branding expert for *Fast Company*'s internationally syndicated blog and is the publisher of *Celebrity Expert Insider*, a monthly newsletter targeting business and brand building strategies.

JW has written over 22 books, including numerous best-sellers, and has been inducted into the National Academy of Best-Selling Authors. JW is married to Linda, his wife of 39 years, and they have two daughters, two granddaughters and two Yorkies. JW is a 6th generation Floridian and splits his time between his home in Orlando and beach house on the Florida west coast.

CHAPTER 11

DEVELOPING A PERSONALIZED POA (PLAN OF ACTION)

BY LYNN LEACH

Ever notice the high rate of attrition in network marketing/mlm groups? I have, and I have to wonder...WHY? I do not believe that people join programs to invest and then drop out three, four or five months down the road. I believe they join programs because they have HOPE and DESIRE. I believe they join programs to improve their circumstances and to achieve some goals. I think the problem is two-fold. First, most network marketers do not have a Plan of Action, and second, they do not have knowledge in marketing. In other words – they simply do not know what to do. In general, those who are new to the industry quit because they are frustrated that they do not understand HOW TO BUILD their business. I believe that direct sales, network marketing and MLM (multi-level marketing) can fit into anyone's lifestyle comfortably, if they are taught to develop a POA (Plan Of Action) and then guided in training for the marketing strategies they select to use.

I have found that there are three keys to directing someone to build a firm foundation in a home-based business that will lead them to success. The three keys are:

1. Developing a personalized Plan Of Action

2. Designing the Plan of Action to fit COMFORTABLY into their lifestyle

3. Implementing a structured training program to teach them how to use the POA

Mary Kay Ash taught me to plan my work and work my plan. A POA will help you to do just that. So let me show you what a POA would consist of with my:

EIGHT STEPS TO DESIGNING A PERSONALIZED POA

<u>STEP ONE</u>

Answer these 11 questions:

1. What is the desire of your heart? Be detailed in your answer. If money were no object, what is it that you desire?

2. What are your goals? Goals are different from the desires. Goals always have a time frame to them. Where do you see yourself at certain points down the road? What is it that you would like to accomplish within certain time frames?

   a. Short range goals
      (i). 6 months
      (ii). 1 year

   b. Mid-range goals
      (i). 2 – 5 years

   c. Long range goals
      (i). 5 – 10 years

3. How much time do you have to invest in your business? We all have different schedules, time constraints, commitments and responsibilities. Will you be working on a hobby basis, part time, or full time? Determine exactly how much time you can CONSISTENTLY dedicate to building your business.

4. What is the financial commitment you can COMFORTABLY afford on a monthly basis? Again, we are all different, and some have a little money to work with, some have no money to work with and some have a lot of money to work with. You can still

work a home-based business no matter where you fall here. If your funds are very restricted and you have nothing to work with, you need to be creative in generating some funding or be willing to put more time and effort into building with the free marketing strategies. It may just take you a little more time to build, but you can still be successful.

5. What talents do you possess? Talents are gifts you are born with, and you can use these in your business. We are all gifted with varied gifts – make yours work to your advantage.

6. What skills have you acquired? We have all acquired different skills from our work and life experiences. Write your skills down. But remember: Talents you are born with, skills you acquire. And if you are open and teachable, you can learn any skills you do not already possess.

7. What strengths do you bring to your business? We all have strengths, so mark yours down so you know what you have to work with.

8. What weak areas do you have that will need special attention to improve? Wisdom dictates that you identify the weak areas you have so you can concentrate on developing them into strengths.

9. Determine if you are a task-oriented person or a people-oriented person. This will help you in determining your marketing strategies so that you are working within a realm of comfort for the way you prefer to work.

10. What are your work preferences? Variety is the spice of life and we are all designed and wired differently. There are literally hundreds of ways to market a product or a service. Those marketing techniques fall into 4 categories, with many different sub divisions within each category. This is an important step. A lot of time you hear people saying that you have to step outside of your comfort zone, and that you need to stretch your people to step outside of their comfort zone. Let me just say that I do not subscribe to that train of thought for new people. For up and coming leaders – yes. But think about this: if you have a brand new person beginning a home-based business with no

experience at all, and you try to make them do things that are outside of their comfort zone, they will NOT be comfortable, they will NOT do the work, they will NOT make the money and therefore they drop out and quit a few months down the road. And for those that think "their way is THE ONLY way to market," all I can say is…SERIOUSLY!!???!! That makes no sense to me. God wired us all differently. I believe it would be foolish for me to demand that everyone on my team work their business exactly the way I work mine. Some people love to work on the phone, while others cannot pick up the 1-ton receiver. Some people like to work on the computer, and some people do not even own a computer. So here are the four major work preferences to select from:

A. Face-to-Face (some call it belly-to-belly marketing). There are so many ways to work this – one on one, groups, party plan, hotel meetings, table and booth events, etc.

B. Phone. There are many ways to utilize phone work.

C. Computer. There are countless ways to market on the computer.

D. Communications though mailings. Direct mail marketing is a huge industry. There are many ways you can utilize mail-marketing strategies.

11. And finally, what is your passion? Passion is different than desire. Maybe you have a passion for working with unwed mothers, or abused women. Perhaps you are passionate about helping animals, or you are concerned over the environment. Some people like to help victims of aids, while others like to work with seniors and still others like to work with babies. Some people want to help children in third world countries have safer drinking water. Those are just a few things that you could be passionate about. So why would that be important in determining a POA? Let me ask you this: If I could show you a way to tie your passion in with your business, how powerful would that be?

STEP TWO

Developing your schedule:

"Plan your work and work your plan" is the greatest wisdom that can be imparted to a business owner. Many of us work a home-based business to gain extra time and freedom. So let's see if we are accomplishing that. I would like you to grab a pen and paper and write down what your priorities are and list them in the order of importance to you.

I am inserting a sample weekly time planner for you to visualize. This particular sample is good because it shows all of the different things you might need to block time out for.

So go ahead and take a weekly time planner and block off all of your commitments. If you work a job, block it off. If you have to spend time traveling to your job, account for that. If you teach Sunday school, block it out. If you belong to a bowling league, block it out. Block out any time you spend cooking or doing laundry or taking care of house chores. Account for time spent with family, your significant other and any personal time you take for yourself to exercise or meditate. Block off absolutely everything you do. Now the times that are NOT blocked are the times you have to build your business. Take some colored highlighters and color code the time you have blocked. Now, hold your weekly time planner out at arms length and check the colors to see if it reflects the priorities you wrote down. Nine times out of ten, the sheet does not reflect you are living your life according to the priorities you have listed.

Use the time sheet to schedule your time for building your business to the point where you can move your priorities into proper alignment with how you want to live your life. The goal is to have balance in your life so your life will run smoothly, stress-free and peacefully. Check a color-coded weekly time sheet each month to evaluate how you are working towards achieving balance in your life and how you are moving towards having priorities in their proper order.

STEP THREE

Setting your budget:

You will need to determine how much money you have to work with on a monthly basis so you can set up your budget. You will need to budget for your start-up costs which includes your initial order and set up fees for your marketing system, your monthly order, and whatever marketing strategies you are selecting. Set your budget up according to percentages. You will not write yourself a paycheck until you reach certain goals within your budget. The first goal is to recoup your initial investment. The second goal is to have your business operating so that it is covering the monthly costs. And the third goal is to be in the profit column.

Once in profit, set aside a certain percentage to reinvest into your business so it can grow on a continual basis, and then write yourself a paycheck. As you reinvest into your business, it grows, and so do your paychecks.

STEP FOUR

Developing your first 6-month plan of action:

Determine how much money you need to generate on a monthly basis and it will help you to determine what you need to do on a monthly basis, a weekly basis and a daily basis. You can even break it down to what you need to do on an hourly basis. In order to do this, you will need to understand the numbers. This is a numbers game. You will need to monitor your closing ratio, and by the way - it will change. Practice does make perfect, and you will see your ratio improving as you consistently take action and master the art of closing. You will need to know how many leads you need to generate to achieve the number of hot prospects you need to have, in order to make one sale of your product or sign one rep up for your team.

You will want to schedule your time according to your marketing strategies, which are determined by the budget you have to work with, your work preferences and your personal schedule.

STEP FIVE

Select your marketing strategies:

There are hundreds, if not thousands of ways to market a product or a service. Select a handful, 3 -5 ways you are comfortable with – you won't want to put all of your eggs in one basket. Your selections will be determined by the ratio of hours you can work, taking into consideration your marketing dollars in your budget and accounting for your preferences.

Next, get the training to understand the strategy you have selected, practice it and master the technique. In addition to marketing strategies, you will also want to select a marketing system to work with. There are free marketing strategies and systems, low cost marketing strategies and systems, medium cost marketing strategies and systems and high cost marketing strategies and systems. Begin where your budget allows you comfortably, and adjust as you reinvest in your business.

Here are some examples of strategies you might select:

- Live meetings
- Classified Ads
- Blogging
- Article Marketing
- Traffic Exchanges
- Radio Marketing
- Press Releases

- Email Campaigns
- Solo Ads
- Table and Booth Events
- Fliers
- Joint Venture Partnerships
- Referrals
- Road Side Signs
- Pay Per Click
- E-zine Advertising
- Banner Exchanges
- Text Ads
- Newspaper Ads
- Phone Blasts
- Cold Calling
- Warm Market
- Sizzle Cards
- SEO Marketing
- Post Cards
- Posters
- Social Media
- IM Marketing (Skype)
- Mobile Marketing
- Video Marketing

(…And this does not even scratch the surface of the hundreds of ways to market.)

STEP SIX

Educate yourself:

Educate yourself about your company, your comp plan and your products. And then be certain to concentrate on studying and mastering the marketing strategies you have selected. But be careful here, it is easy to become overwhelmed. I suggest you start with one strategy, practice it and master it and then add a second one. Do not try to swallow the whole elephant in one bite. It will overwhelm you and burn you out. Pace yourself.

STEP SEVEN

Track and Evaluate:

TRACK EVERYTHING YOU DO, so you know where to spend your time and money most effectively. There are many tracking systems on the Internet, both no cost and low cost. If you are working off line, developing a local market and generating local leads, just set up a code system for yourself. For example, if you are using roadside signs (some call them bandit signs), and you are using a sizzle line to send them too, just put a special code on the road side sign so you can evaluate how a certain message or ad is pulling, and then ask them to leave the code number when they leave their name and phone number. When you do your follow-up call to them, ask them where they saw your sign, so you can evaluate which intersections pull the best. You can set up tracking systems for any kind of marketing you are doing, both online and offline. Evaluate and adjust on a regular basis. You will also want to track your time and efforts so you can evaluate your work and your efforts and adjust as necessary.

Weekly Goals and Activity Tracking Sheet — Qinternational

Activities:	Sunday Actual	Goal	Monday Actual	Goal	Tuesday Actual	Goal	Wednesday Actual	Goal	Thursday Actual	Goal	Friday Actual	Goal	Saturday Actual	Goal	Totals Actual	Goal
Contacts																
Invts/Appts																
Presentations																
Demos																
Samples																
3 way calls																
Follow-Ups																
Results:																
Sales #/$'s																
New Reps																
New BV																
New MO's																
New Custs																
New CPV																

My Goals for this Week > Title: _____ 3 Level GV: _____ PV: _____ CPV: _____ Check: $_____

To achieve my goals, I am helping the following Reps to achieve their Goals:

_____ _____ _____
_____ _____ _____

STEP EIGHT

Make your adjustments and formulate a one-year plan of action:

Once you work a 6-month plan of action you have a base to formulate future plans from. Change what isn't working, step up what is working.

To summarize, TRUTHFULLY answer the questions outlined in step one, and share them with your upline business partner or mentor. This way they will be equipped to give you the best business advice when mentoring you. Once you have your questions answered from step one, develop your Plan Of Action according to your answers. Then be DISCIPLINED and COMMITTED in taking daily action to create amazing results. You create the roadmap to your own success. And remember: HE WHO MARKETS BEST – WINS!

PLAN YOUR WORK AND WORK YOUR PLAN!

BE DISCIPLINED!!

BE COMMITTED!!!

BE SUCCESSFUL!!!!

About Lynn

Lynn has been married to her husband Norman for 41 years, and they have 3 sons and 6 granddaughters.

She has been involved in direct sales / network marketing for 45 years. She also has 13 years of experience in restaurant management. Her 44 years of ministry include serving on the board of directors in leadership positions for 8 large organizations and also 3 national secular non-profit organizations. She served as pastor of Mars Hill Baptist Church and was a gospel clown and had a puppet ministry. She now uses network marketing as a ministry to help families, ministers and missionaries, and as a fundraiser to help non-profit organizations and churches.

Marketing and teaching are two of Lynn's strengths, and she has developed her own training program to help people understand how to build their home businesses.

Because she understands what a toxic world we live in, she has embraced the Q philosophy of maintaining our life essentials — our air, water and nutrition. She was the first to achieve the rank of Premier, the highest position in Q International, Inc.

Lynn is passionate about all natural healing — on all levels: physical, emotional, relational, spiritual and financial.

She owns Common Scents Health Research & Wellness Centers and is an aromatherapist and massage therapist. She specializes in essential oil science concentrating on emotional release, all-natural pain management and all-natural first aide.

You can reach Lynn at 724-292-8481 or email her at: pastorlynn@comcast.net. Her website is: www.mentorwithlynn.com

CHAPTER 12

CHANGING BAD HABITS

BY MICHELLE A. BATES

If I know nothing else, I know all about the journey and eventual victory of changing bad habits. On my individual journey, I also learned that "bad habits" are a sure way to sabotage any chance of success.

Allow me to share a little of my journey with you. A few years ago, I found an amazing office space. The location could not be better, there was free parking, a beautiful lobby, a comfortable waiting area, a relaxing break room, and the office space itself was spectacular! The whole package was nothing short of impressive. And I absolutely loved the office receptionist, Beth. All of this was mine for the taking for less than the cost of a cup of coffee per day. I would have been crazy to pass it up, right. Beth made it clear to me, in no uncertain terms, that the price was not a misprint and that I should be very mindful of the fact the office space would not be available at that price for very long. Wow, was that an understatement! I knew quite well what I had found and I also knew at that very moment, standing in the reception area, that this was my new office.

Everything felt right with the world. I was home. I distinctly remember hearing the words to a song from Young Frankenstein echoing through my head, "Oh…at last I have found you." I remember Beth smiling at me saying, "Yes honey, you belong here and I just can't wait to work with you." I assured her I would be in touch within the next twenty-four hours and, as I stepped into the elevator, I imagined what it would feel like to be entering and leaving my very own office on a daily basis. I was at peace, it was such a beautiful day, and I felt like life just could not get any better than this. I wasn't just dreaming anymore...I was finally taking action. I was making my dream a reality.

Absolutely nothing could bring me down on that day or stand in my way. So, in my ignorant bliss, I bounced through the clouds to see a very close friend of mine whose opinion I valued greatly. In hindsight, I realize this friend was also one of the most negative people I knew. I guess that a part of me just needed validation. I wanted this person to be as proud of me as I was of myself at that moment. When we first met up, I got the exact feedback and excitement from my friend that I had so hoped I would get. He told me how proud he was of me and raved about my courage and strength. He stroked my ego further by telling me that if anyone could make this work, it would be me. To have my friend's support fed me with energy. I just knew I was making the right move.

Then came the kick in the gut, "You know Michelle," he said, "I know I encouraged you and said you can do this, but don't you think it's kind of risky?" I had come to learn that the truth always comes after the "but". He went on to say, "You are new here and I was just thinking you don't exactly have any clients here yet." My heart instantly sank as I thought but dared not say, "What am I supposed to do?" Get clients and say, "I don't have anywhere to meet with you yet, but hey! I'll give ya' a call when I do." I simply continued to sit and listen to my friend go on and on about why it was probably not a good Idea. The final blow was when he said, "I understand that this is important to you, but maybe you should consider the fact that you're older now. Working for yourself is risky and maybe your best bet is to work for somebody else. It's less risky. I work for someone else. Does that mean I'm a failure?"

I told my friend he absolutely was not a failure. He was doing what made him happy. I explained that I've worked for other people and I learned as much as I could from the experience. I further shared with him that I felt it was now time for me to do what would make me happy, and that was to work for myself. On that note, I graciously excused myself and went home. I sat up all night and thought about all of the mixed emotions of the day. I went from walking on clouds to skydiving toward the ground without a parachute.

The next day came and Beth was expecting me. She had left me a message reminding me about coming in. **Enter** bad habit...Stage left. Negative self-talk. I began asking myself, "What are you doing?" I told myself, "It will never work." "You're new here and you have no clients" kept echoing in my head. "If it doesn't work out everyone will think you're a failure," a script embedded in me for many years. "Maybe you would be better off working for someone else". I could not get rid of the doubt and negative feedback from my friend, what if he was right.

I called Beth and told her I was going to have to give it a little more thought. She indicated that she understood but again reminded me that at that price she wouldn't be able to hold on to it. Nor did she think any other office in the building would be inexpensively-priced. Her words still ring in my ears, "Don't wait too long Michelle." Well, wait was exactly I did. I waited and waited. Finally, I got up the courage and confidence once again and decided to take the risk. I called Beth, only to find out that the space had indeed been rented. Beth was right. Not only was the office rented, but also no other office has leased at that price since! My procrastination gremlin led to a missed opportunity that would not come around again for three years. And for three years all I could think of was how I was a ready and willing participant to join the ranks of the most successful people in the world...and I blew it!

Procrastination, that bad habit I thought I had permanently rid myself of had reared its ugly head once again. Where did I go wrong? Why did I revert back to this habit? Then it dawned on me. . . I had never truly gotten rid of it. Sure, I changed how I did a few things and got some good results. I had begun to take action as opposed to putting things off until later. I managed my time better. I even started to get more sleep. I had made some positive changes. The problem was that not only had I neglected to acknowledge the power of my triggers, I was also relying on willpower alone and was still vulnerable to what others thought instead of trusting my own judgment.

When forced to take a long hard look at myself, I realized that my approach was all wrong. In order to change my bad habits, I had to change from the inside out. I had to change my philosophy. I had to truly believe in myself and what I could accomplish. This was the day I knew that if I were to get what I wanted out of this short life, if I was ever truly going to be successful, things had to change!

The steps I took next changed my life forever. First, I got a notebook and a pen and found a quiet place where I could reflect. Next, I thought long and hard about what my goals were and wrote them all down. I made sure to make them "SMART" – Specific, measurable, attainable, realistic and timely. For example, during this whole ordeal I had put on a couple pounds. One of my goals was to lose them, so instead of simply saying, "I want to lose weight," my goal was "I weigh 138 pounds by May 28th." Having a list of my goals would also prove to be helpful in that some of my smaller goals could act as replacements for my bad habits.

Next I took a hard look at what was holding me back and wrote those things down. This list consisted of my bad habits. I had already learned from my journey that it is wise to work on only one bad habit at a time, so I picked one. One that I considered to be the most harmful to my road to success — procrastination. Now it was time to figure out what causes me to procrastinate. What my triggers were. This was a crucial step because, if I could identify my triggers, I could come up with ways to fight them and eliminate this bad habit forever. My list of triggers included distractions and lack of focus, fear, and needing approval from those close to me. I had a few triggers listed, but for the sake of not boring you to death, we will stick with these three.

After identifying my triggers it was important to list ways to battle them.

(I). What was I feeling when I felt distracted or unable to focus? The answer, I was overwhelmed. I had a lot on my plate and I had to learn to deal with it better. In my mind, I had started managing my time better but I still had six kids, a home to manage, and a business to run. I had to learn to give myself a break. My biggest problem was that I never said no…to anyone! I said yes to the kids, my clients, my friends…heck, even to people I didn't really know. I could write a book on "knowing when to say no" but, to keep this short and sweet, I had to come up with a comeback line to all of the "Michelle, could you ...?" So instead of saying yes, I decided to start saying "I would love to help you. Let me check my calendar/schedule and I'll get back to you." If the task I was being asked to perform was mutually productive, then I would try to find time to do it. However, what I found was that more often than not I was being asked to do things that were helping everyone else achieve their goals and keeping me from reaching my own.

In cases like these I would get back to the person within twenty-four hours and very nicely decline. There, problem solved. And yes, it worked like a charm. Even though I had stopped putting so much on my plate, I knew that there would still be times when I felt overwhelmed. I needed a backup plan, so for those times I would sit still and meditate for about 10 minutes, or if it were possible I'd do some jumping jacks, push-ups and squats (this is where my list of goals came in handy).

(II). Next trigger, fear. I had to ask myself what I was feeling when I was afraid. Well, I was afraid of failure – afraid of what people would say or think. This fear would lead me to negative self-talk like, "What if this was the biggest mistake of my life?"…or, "I can't do this, I'm not good enough." Now, "I" was the enemy. My negative thoughts and my lack of confidence in my ability to succeed had taken over. This is when I realized that the only way to deal with fear is to embrace it. If I could do that, I could better deal with it. I had to be more mindful of the things I would tell myself. And this is where affirmations come in to play. Affirmations are a wonderful tool for building self-esteem. When creating them I was sure they were short, positive and written in the present tense, For example, if I notice myself saying something like, "I can't do this," I would immediately conquer those negative thoughts by affirming and assuring myself that "I am confident and successful and I achieve all of my goals." I would repeat my affirmation over and over again until I felt strong and capable of doing just that… achieving my goals.

(III). As far as my last trigger, seeking others approval, that's where I had to take full responsibility for my actions. No one had to like, agree or even believe in what I was doing except me. I have full control over my thoughts and my actions, yet I was giving other people my power. The truth is that if I had believed in myself and what I was doing, my friend could never have made me second guess myself to the point of self-sabotage. I had spent years viewing myself through the eyes of others and the time to stop was now.

So you see, the formula for changing bad habits is quite simple:

1. Acknowledge they exist.

2. Write down your goals.

3. Identify what keeps you from reaching your goals and you will have a list of your bad habits.

4. Find out what your triggers are. What happens or how do you feel just before performing you bad habit.

5. Come up with ways to fight these triggers (remember to use affirmations and smaller goals).

6. Follow these steps constantly for twenty-one to twenty-eight days. They say it take twenty-one days to break/form a habit. I found great success in following all of these steps consistently for twenty-eight to thirty days. Sure I had slip ups, but I didn't give up and that is where the constancy came in. More importantly, you must have a deep desire to change. You must truly believe that change is possible. Without this, you can follow the steps all you want but you will surely fail. Your foundation must be built upon desire and belief.

You can change your bad habits and achieve the success you want – and remember, you are always and in all ways, greater than you think you are!

About Michelle

Michelle is a Lifestyle, Fitness and Nutrition Coach in St Petersburg, Florida. She has been coaching others on living an overall healthy lifestyle for over 12 years.

Michelle attended the National Personal Trainers Institute in Orlando FL, where she graduated and became a Certified Personal Trainer and Nutrition Consultant. She also sat for the National Sports and Conditioning Association's exam and earned their certification as a Personal Trainer.

Through dedication and hard work, Michelle learned everything she could about proper diet and exercise. Michelle's passion for fitness quickly turned into a lifestyle after the birth of her fourth child. Weighing in at 172 pounds, up 42 pounds from her usual 130, she knew she had to make a change. She quickly learned that resistance training, whether using body weight, bands or dumbbells was not just for men. Michelle also learned that women too could lift and still look like women; Not only that, "but the benefits of doing so in addition to cardiovascular exercise and proper diet were absolutely priceless!"

As a busy mother of six, Michelle knows how difficult it is for men and women alike to take the time to exercise and eat properly. One thing she educates her clients on is the fact that fitness is a lifestyle. It is something that you must incorporate into your daily schedule and make a habit.

Michelle's personal training programs are customized and are based on your goals, level of experience, needs, and lifestyle. Very much like personal training programs, fitness and nutrition coaching is customized and based on the clients' goals, level of experience, needs, and lifestyle. It is a perfect choice for those who do not need a personal trainer but need guidance on weight loss, nutrition and an exercise program.

Michelle is also a dynamic, knowledgeable and enthusiastic speaker. Her speaking engagements focus on life-transforming techniques that will leave her audience with the knowledge they need to achieve and maintain the lives and bodies they've always wanted.

To learn more about Michelle visit: www.michelleabates.com or call 727-755-4348.

CHAPTER 13

FROM FARM BOY TO WEALTH ADVISOR
— HOW TO ACHIEVE WILD SUCCESS <u>AND</u> SLEEP WELL AT NIGHT

BY MONTGOMERY TAYLOR

Believe it or not, "success" in business is not about grabbing all the money you can, as fast as you can. Money is just the result of the value your customers place on your product or service. Therefore, your effort must be directed to the value you can bring to your customer.

Let me illustrate what I mean and how it is relevant to your success by telling you the story of my own business success and the steps that I've found helpful. I'll start by telling you about a client…

A retired, single woman came to see me for some financial advice. I asked her how I could be of help. She was concerned about running out of money some day. Her investment account balances kept declining and she felt helpless. I asked her why she didn't just ask her current advisor to make her investments more conservative. She told me how each time she went to the advisor to discuss her concerns, he would give her a hug and some smooth talk and she'd walk out feeling reassured—until she got home, anyway. She liked her advisor, but realized his approach was a lot like a stereotypical used car salesman.

I discovered that this smooth advisor had really just transferred her money into various accounts without any connection to a financial plan. No wonder she was so nervous about her financial security! Her advisor wasn't looking at the big picture of how to really help her and improve her whole financial situation. Success, for this advisor, was all about making a quick product sale and improving his bottom line. Fortunately, I was able to help this woman put a meaningful financial plan in place, giving her peace of mind. She remains a satisfied client of mine these eight years hence.

That advisor has since crashed and burned—his concept of success couldn't keep him in business. I would like to share with you a business model based on good behavior; I firmly believe that in order to succeed in business (as a financial advisor in my case), you must put your clients' best interests ahead of your own.

THE WAY I SEE IT, YOU'RE EITHER A TRUSTED ADVISOR OR YOU'RE A SALESMAN

I'm not bashing salesmen here—just pointing out the important difference in positioning, mindset and approach when you're advising someone about their financial security as opposed to selling someone a vacuum cleaner.

Let me stop for a moment and explain my background and perspective on trust. My mom and dad were kids during the Great Depression. My dad served in the Navy during World War II and my mom worked in a factory making supplies for the war effort. My dad came home with many medals on his chest to attest to his bravery. Those medals were added to all the medals he earned as a Boy Scout in his youth.

After the war, Dad married Mom and then went to work for the California Highway Patrol. He worked the night shift so he could spend the days working our farm in the beautiful Alexander Valley outside of Healdsburg, California. Mom and Dad started a Cub Scout troop and served as the den mother and father. My two brothers and I, along with all the neighborhood boys, were taught the Scout oath and law with my mom and dad as teachers and role models. Honesty, integrity, a strong work ethic, politeness and respect were discussed and expected.

When I first got into the investment business, I was still living on our family farm. A well-known man who lived in the valley and did some investment work recruited me to come work under his wing. Who wanted investment advice from a twenty-one year old? Well, I didn't have any trouble getting in to talk investments with the neighbors—they all knew my family, our history, and our values, so there was a pre-established level of trust.

Trust was critical from the very beginning and helped me get in the door. Prospective clients never thought for a moment that I was there just to earn a commission; my role was to convince them that I was knowledgeable about the investment and why it might be beneficial for them. When it comes to high cost items and hard-earned money, I've found that people don't want to be 'sold'—they want the assistance of a trusted advisor.

IN ORDER FOR YOU TO SLEEP AT NIGHT, YOUR CLIENTS NEED TO BE ABLE TO SLEEP AT NIGHT

After high school I followed in my father's footsteps and went into law enforcement. I worked at the Sheriff's Department and the Police Department, and I even went to Washington, D.C. and worked in the FBI office. I found it satisfying to be able to protect or help someone. People sleep better knowing that dedicated police officers are patrolling their neighborhood all through the night. I found it honorable to protect and to serve in this fashion. It felt good to stand between some 'bad guy' and their victim or potential victim.

Eventually, I found that fighting with drunks and confronting people who did not want my help was wearing on me. I figured there had to be a better way to provide for my family and work where I could find true satisfaction. Knowing that the FBI would hire people with accounting degrees, I went back to college and pursued a degree in accounting. While taking accounting and tax courses, I took part-time jobs as a stockbroker and as a tax preparer.

The investment business fascinated me. I was drawn by the concepts of compound interest and stock market growth. However, it didn't take long for me to realize that while the brokers I worked with were financially successful, it wasn't because they knew anything smart about investment strategy. It had more to do with being chummy and playing golf with all the right people. It was also plain as day that they

NEW RULES OF SUCCESS

didn't have the ethics my mom and dad had taught me. These were rude awakenings and eye-opening experiences for this young farm boy from Alexander Valley. These brokers were taking advantage of people…and I didn't want their kind of success.

So, rather than crossing the country on a crime fighting mission in hot pursuit of the FBI's 10 Most Wanted (with my cape tucked inconspicuously beneath my suit coat), I chose instead to protect and to serve in the financial arena. I saw a huge need. Elder abuse, identity theft and investment scams regularly make the news. Less visible, but probably more common in my opinion, are cases of incompetent and inadequate financial 'advisors' who cause their clients sleepless nights. These 'advisors' look at their own net income and consider themselves to be successful. But how can they sleep?

So, I suggest that you think of your client as someone who sleeps in the room next door to yours. If they're restless and uneasy, chances are you'll hear about it, especially if it is due to something you did. Do what is right and it gives peace of mind. You'll both sleep better. Even during economic downturns, I sleep well because I know I have done the very best I can for my clients.

HELP YOUR CLIENTS LEAVE A LEGACY—AND LEAVE ONE YOURSELF AS WELL

Quite often when I'm getting to know my clients and understanding their financial objectives, we'll get into a discussion about leaving a legacy. I may even ask them, "What do you want to be remembered for?" If I really want to press them on this issue, I'll ask them, "What would you like your obituary to say?" Have you ever seen a deer in your headlights? That is the look clients give me when I dare ask them that question.

Ideally, though, that is an outstanding approach to financial planning. You start with the end in mind. Wow! What a concept. Give serious thought to where you want to end up in life and what meaning your life should have, and then design a plan to achieve that particular ending. Helping people in this way puts all the emphasis on them and the successful achievement of their goals. It is not about you or the successful selling of some product.

Zig Zigler said that if you really want to succeed in business, just help as many people as you can. I know from experience that if you help people leave a legacy, you'll not only succeed in business, but even better, you'll leave a legacy of your own. So…how do you want your obituary to read?

HERE ARE THE <u>FIVE STEPS TO SUCCESS</u> AS I SEE IT:

1. Be competent
Obviously, you must be competent in the skills required by your chosen profession. Don't make the mistake, however, of attaining the basic education, certifications or experience to perform the job and think you're done. This is really just the foundation. Maintaining your competency, honing your skills, and staying current are ongoing processes—which lead to mastery.

In my own case, obtaining my CPA and CFP certifications was just the beginning. In the twenty-plus years since I hung those credentials on my office wall, I've learned so much. And not just from the annual continuing education requirements or even working in the profession year after year, but in regular and never-ending reading of professional publications and books on the topics important to the building and deepening of my understanding.

It doesn't stop with reading. A natural out-growth of competency and mastery is research, writing and teaching. This is why I've pursued opportunities and not shied away from writing articles and books and teaching on the subjects of my work. It has also been fun, and an honor, to be interviewed for newspaper, radio and television.

2. Be principled
In business school, you probably sat through a class on ethics. Those classes are good and often very interesting, but that is not what I'm talking about here. Every business person needs to have a solid foundation of principles they live by, personally and professionally. Your principles (honesty, integrity, loyalty, generosity, commitment, charity) will be called on regularly in your dealings with clients, co-workers, vendors—everybody really. Your actions will speak volumes. Your honorable deeds will determine the success of your business career.

Almost every day in my business I'm called on to take action where my principles are of extreme importance. Especially in the investment business, it would be very easy to over-charge a client here and there, or not refund some unearned fee. But as with all forms of dishonesty, you have to know that it will come back to bite you. You will be found out and your career will be over.

Trust is earned slowly over time, but can be lost in a moment. Any little gain achieved by unethical behavior will pale in comparison to the wrath you'll bring upon yourself and take to your grave. <u>The Golden Rule:</u> *Do unto others as you would have them do unto you*, is a theme I hold near and dear. I encourage you to do the same.

3. Be transparent

In the financial services industry, unscrupulous advisors have found it easy to scam investors in multiple ways. One way is by preparing fake investment account statements in their own offices and mailing them to the client, making it look like their investment is growing just fine. In reality there is no investment at all. The advisor is using the money to pay for a lifestyle like the rich and famous. Another way advisors scam their clients is by only highlighting the "pros" and passing over the "cons" when introducing investment opportunities.

For this reason, my business uses a third party custodian whose function is to keep the books and independently report directly to the client on all account holdings and transaction activity. The investment activity is completely transparent. Clients can see exactly what is going on by looking at their statements, postmarked from Boston, or by going online to the custodian's website and accessing their accounts directly.

Clients can see my authenticity by how I care for them—with *transparency*.

4. Be focused

The clearer you can be with yourself in determining your long-term career goals, the easier it will be to make the proper decisions today. I know this is a basic "Goal-setting 101" type of statement, but I see it violated by too many people. You don't need to do much reading on success to find that a basic tenet is focus and determination. The world is full of wonderful success stories of people who zeroed in on their objective and wouldn't let up until they achieved success.

My own professional practice has included many ups and downs and years where I banged my head against the wall. Some years weren't very profitable, but I was so bound and determined to succeed that I worked hard and kept at it. I was, and still am, constantly reading technical books and business development books, looking to sharpen my skills and to find new ways of growing my business.

I ultimately realized that the more I focused on bringing value to clients, the more new clients I had coming in. People don't mind paying for a service, as long as they see an equal or greater value coming back. *A good practice is to set a fair and equitable price, and then exceed clients' expectations.*

5. Be helpful

Do you remember when gas stations were "service stations?" And do you remember when you could walk into any store and be greeted by a knowledgeable person who was willing and able to help you? Boy, those were the days.

These days, many businesses seem to go for the low-overhead business model and even rely on their online presence to generate sales. Some customers welcome that format—going to the cheapest dealer, making their purchase, and getting it over with ASAP. My experience is that most customers don't really prefer this method. Instead they have been forced into it by the lack of competent, courteous customer service.

To compete against the bigger financial institutions and all the online services, I've emphasized our local presence and high-touch client service. Old fashioned service with a warm smile is welcomed by those who value their time and appreciate the relationship. I tell new prospective clients that I'll help them just like I help my own Mom.

SUCCESS — A PLAN WITH THE END IN MIND

Over the years I've certainly had my share of opportunities and success. I've built a professional services firm comprised of a team of multi-disciplinary professionals with experience working with individuals and helping them with their financial matters. We manage investments, prepare financial plans, prepare income tax returns and do other strategic financial consulting.

I've been fortunate to have made it to that place in my career where I no longer have 'an axe to grind.' I'm independent and unbiased. I do what I believe in—period. These days, I advise people who want my help, and I teach and write. When I take on a new client it is not because I "need" more business, but because I enjoy helping people who want to be helped, and I know that I can provide valuable advice and service.

All of this became possible because I approached business as I approached life as a young child with beliefs in honesty, integrity, politeness and respect—all character qualities drilled into me on a beautiful country farm by good, salt-of-the-earth parents with a strong work ethic and solid family values.

One last principle I've found to be true, and it's from the Old Testament, has to do with sowing and reaping. In other words, whatever you put in, you get out. Whatever you are reaping today is a result of what you have sown in the past. Your life today, in every respect, is the result of your past decisions and behaviors.

This sowing and reaping principle is a timeless truth. All lasting success, happiness, and high achievement come from organizing your life in harmony with such timeless principles. When you do, you will achieve satisfaction and enjoyment at levels seldom experienced by the average person. You will take complete charge of your destiny and achieve the success you planned.

About Montgomery

Montgomery Taylor was named **"The Only CPA We Trust"** by KZST Radio. They chose him to be the tax expert for KZST listeners. Mr. Taylor is past president of the Redwood Empire Estate Planning Council, and a frequent speaker for the California Institute of Retirement and Estate Planning. He is a recognized expert on wealth management and featured in newspapers, magazines, radio and television.

In August 2012, his book, *Before It's Too Late ~ Retirement and Estate Solutions*, was published and has received wonderful praise and reviews by local business leaders and professional reviewers. Mr. Taylor was also interviewed on *The Patti Gribow* television talk-show, which airs on the Comcast Hometown Network.

His 34-year career in financial services first began as a Stockbroker, then as a Certified Public Accountant, Certified Financial Planner, Certified IRA Distribution Specialist, and Registered Investment Advisor. His considerable experience includes four years with Pisenti & Brinker, CPAs, a prestigious regional Northern California Accounting and Advisory Firm, where he learned to integrate complex tax decisions with personal financial planning. This was followed by seven years with the Sonoma County Employees Retirement Association (SCERA), where he learned first-hand what it's like to manage a $700 million Pension Trust. Mr. Taylor has spent the past fifteen years building his own CPA firm, Montgomery Taylor, CPA, and a separate investment management company, Montgomery Taylor and Company, LLC.

Mr. Taylor's firm is independent and offers unbiased advice with a holistic approach to wealth management and prosperity. With his comprehensive experience in personal and institutional money management, tax planning, and investment decision-making, he has the unique ability to sort through all the conventional retirement planning wisdom and pick out the parts you can depend on.

To learn more about Montgomery Taylor, visit: www.TaxWiseAdvisor.com
Or call (707) 576-8700.

CHAPTER 14

THE FIRST RULE OF SUCCESS IS MANAGING STRESS!

BY KATRINA LUISE EVERHART, RYT

Stress like the weather is a constant in everyone's life. Like the weather, each person tolerates different conditions in their own way. Stress can be the same as the weather in our lives; tolerable at times, intolerable at other times. Like the weather, we cannot control what happens to us. Unlike the weather, we can do something about the way we react to events and our stress. Active people have more stress, mainly because they are active. Too much activity and stress, folks become ill. Common indications that we are not dealing with stress well often come in the form of diseases.

DISEASES RELATED TO STRESS

Stress-related diseases include shingles, styes, eczema, muscle spasms, hypothyroidism, genital herpes in women, psoriasis, rosacea, fibromyalgia, cold sores, dry mouth, panic attacks, temporomandibular joint disorder (or TMJ), thrush, hair loss, acne, vitiligo, indigestion, Hodgkin's disease, cystic fibrosis, canker sores, Cushing's disease, bruxism, eye strain, insomnia, dystonia, dysthymia, stiff-person syndrome, asthma complexities, cyclic vomiting syndrome (or CVS), besides high blood pressure, migraine headaches, and heart disease. Stress aggravates pain and issues with Irritable Bowel Syndrome (or IBS), Multiple Sclerosis (or

MS), Post Traumatic Stress Disorder (or PTSD), heart disease, diabetes, Chronic Obstructive pulmonary disease (or COPD), and cancer, to name a few.

Common laments in professional and personal situations include desires to have stress disappear. Avoiding stress is like trying to avoid the weather, it is unrealistic. Muscles form based on weight and resistance. Weight and resistance create stress on the muscle. As the muscle pushes against the stress, the muscle grows bigger.

TOO LITTLE STRESS

Stress is necessary to grow. Physically, without an appropriate amount of weight and resistance, blood clots form, bones become brittle, and muscles get weak. Women who do not exercise and eat properly often get osteoporosis. A study of 80-year-old women in a nursing home using soup cans as weights discovered within 8 weeks of using weights, the women slowed osteoporosis progression. A Siberian Orphanage documentary noted children in cribs until five and six years of age were unable to walk. Their legs were unable to hold them up. Young or old, not enough weight on the bones causes problems.

NO STRESS

No stress creates health problems as well. Deep Vein Thrombosis is common for individuals who sit too long whether they are in an office chair, a home recliner, or an airplane. Nicknamed Bedsores, the lack of movement creates sores where a bone presses an object. Depression and anxiety are common for those who do not have any stress in their lives, along with disease.

TOO MUCH STRESS IS BAD;
TOO LITTLE STRESS IS ALSO BAD

Each person has their own level of acceptable stress, colloquially referred to as **balance!** Balancing stress relates not only to our own actions which interact with others, but also to our reactions to occurrences that are out of our control. Focusing on time management and planning activities, within reason, help manage the issues we have with unexpected occurrences.

TIME MANAGEMENT

Time Management is not just determining a daily list of required tasks. It means thinking about our mission or philosophy overall, of life. Done correctly, identifying objectives, listing goals, and determining tasks, help achieve goals regularly, and lessen stress. Half of all folks do not make New Year's Resolutions. Of those who make New Year's Resolutions, 90% abandon them within 30 days. One of the main reasons for abandoning a New Year's resolution is time. Certainly, many may be busy and the resolution may have been frivolous. Yet, this is the same thing that happens to folks who do not achieve goals or even set goals. These folks often wonder why they are not successful. Time management is key not only to daily life, but also to achieving goals, and success over a lifetime. Saying "No" is just as important as "Yes!"

SUCCESS IN THE DICTIONARY IS THE ONLY PLACE IT OCCURS BEFORE WORK!

Success requires us to manage our time and not the tasks to get by on a daily basis. In exercise, we do better when we exercise around the same time every day. This in no way means that we do the same exercise or have the same routine every day! Just as our body becomes used to certain activities; the more likely you perform the same daily activities means you will hit a plateau, whether it be in weight loss, a job, in personal hobbies, or relationships. Yet, we cannot become erratic in our behavior as this creates stress for us, and others.

Plateaus stop your progress whether in weight loss or in the job market. Stress is a part of success. We cannot achieve success immediately. And we cannot deal with all stressful situations successfully without managing our time, actions, decisions, language, thoughts, emotions, and reactions. Time management and using a specific decision-making process helps us practice, learn, do, and achieve.

WORK AND SUCCESS!

Action works best when dealing with stress. Yet, the wrong actions can be devastating. Think about road rage and the person who is stressed from something that happens at work. Cutting people off and causing accidents on the way home does not change problems at work. Folks who do not have specific goals, who do not use a time management

141

and decision-making system are accidents waiting to happen. While the right actions lead to solutions, the wrong actions become a safety issue for most.

Success requires that we manage our eating, sleep, exercise, professional, community, and personal activities. Eating, sleep, and exercise are keys to our ability to enjoy any success we achieve. Too much fat, sugar, and salt causes health problems beyond just issues with headaches, heart disease, liver, weight, and kidney problems. All slow our memory and increase our cortisol. Cortisol is one of the stress hormones. Cortisol tells your body to hold onto fat! Ever heard a person say, I exercise an hour a day and cannot lose weight. In many cases, they are eating high levels of fat and drinking a lot of caffeine.

STRESS AND SLEEP: INSOMNIA OR NARCOLEPSY

Sleep disturbances ranging from insomnia to narcolepsy, are often stress related! In 2010, $2 billion dollars were spent purchasing over-the-counter sleep medications! Popular sleep medications whether over-the-counter or prescription should not to be used more than three months. Besides dependence, overuse creates issues like sleepwalking, sleep working, driving, and eating. One popular prescription sleep medication caught the attention of the FDA in 2013. Due to various accidents, the allowed limits have been drastically reduced. Examples of problems made the news! One paper reported a woman drove 600 miles before she woke up; another one reported the person setting her house on fire.

At some point, we all have trouble sleeping. One common myth is drinking hot milk! Yes, it has tryptophan, which aids in sleep, but it occurs in such small amounts, that it does not really help. Granted some report always drinking milk before bed and falling asleep immediately. This is due to the **routine or time management system**. The body becomes used to certain triggers. Unlike exercise, which becomes less effective over time, a pattern before bed increases the likelihood of triggering sleep. A regular bedtime and a regular routine before bed help folks sleep better. Time management is not just between 8 am and 5 pm or 8 am to 8 pm with school and work, ignoring personal, social, and community events. Time management is 24/7!

MEMORY

Stress, insomnia, lack of exercise, as well as fatty foods degrades memory. Anytime your memory suffers, you will have problems achieving success, personally, and/or professionally. Exercise, healthy eating, managing stress, and sleeping will help memory. Each person's ability to exercise will vary based on their ability and goals. The less stressed our body is, the better it reacts to stressful situations. Exercise does help deal with stress and our bodies reactions to stress, in the right amounts.

PRODUCTIVITY AND DECISION MAKING

Less stress increases your productivity; less stress increases your ability to make better decisions! Decision-making is a part of time management. Using a specific, systematic decision process, and not making spur of the moment decisions, lessens stress. Productive decision-making requires defining the problem, recognizing at least three or four different sides of the situation, not just one, identifying the constraints, and doing some research before seeking feedback. Certainly, a simple **Pros and Cons** method, popularized by Benjamin Franklin in the 1700s is common. It is a good method when you have one or two basic choices and no other issues or compounding factors. It is great for selecting a can of peas at the grocer's and other similar simple decisions.

Similar to a pros and cons, is **Force Field Analysis**. Instead of two columns as in the pros and cons, you have three. Column one records the forces <u>for</u> change; the second has the forces <u>against</u> change. In the third, you determine whether the force is weak or strong. Then you evaluate the importance and make your selection(s) based on the forces strength or weaknesses for change. A **Grid Analysis** allows the options to be rank ordered, while a **Cost/Benefit Analysis** determines the costs/benefits based on the strength or weakness of costs.

For more complex issues requiring comparisons, a **Paired Comparison Analysis** allows you to rank order issues or changes, and determine alternative solutions based on the strength or weakness of the choices. A **Pareto Analyses** provides a score for the most important factors, thus allowing those complex issues to have an order to the decisions based on priorities. And, for complex objectives which need to occur over time, a **Decision Tree Analysis** allows for choices to be ranked at each level. Playing Devil's Advocate or "What if" as long as you review a variety of positive and negative options, lessens fear of the unknown(s) and stress.

Using the **Six Hats Thinking Method** can help when different folks are involved in decisions. Each hat: white, red, black, yellow, green, and blue have a different focus. White focuses on data; Red focuses on emotions; Black focuses on the negative; Yellow focuses on the positive, Green creates new alternatives; and Blue maintains the process, not allowing things to become too negative or too positive, and ensuring that there is enough information to make decisions.

Decision-making requires us to think clearly. The less stressed we are, the more able we are to understand the forces, challenges, choices, and changes that need to be made in our decision-making. As we spend at least some time thinking about the choices and determine their positive or negative benefits based on our mission in life, our objectives and goals, it helps us become more successful. **Basically, better decisions lead to less Stress and more Success!**

VENTING IS BAD FOR YOUR HEALTH

Stress worsens when you vent! While a common suggestion, venting makes matters worse. Popularized by media, venting became known as action necessary to help relieve stress. Research found the opposite! Stress was determined in the research by increases in blood pressure, heart rate, and angry feelings. Hitting objects, yelling, screaming, and using profanities only dramatize the way individuals view problems – increasing anxiety, anger, and aggression, whether overt or covert. **Bottom line; venting increases aggression and stress!**

Adversarial types of exercise also increase the anxiety and stress. Adversarial types include boxing or any sport where one person or a group become villains in the process to be destroyed or beaten. Basic exercise reduces stress, if it is the right type of exercise. Activities where the person is able to be active and deal with the issues without harming themselves or others, decrease stress.

Changing the environment helps relieve stress. Some folks do handy work such as carve or whittle wood, knit, weave, or paint; others scrub floors and clean their house, while others may do yard work, play a game of tennis, golf, basketball, or do a singular activity like walk, run, or meditate. Cooking can be good or bad; good, because it can be a great activity, bad, because folks can easily overeat. Overuse of one type of activity can become stressful. Just as we have different stressors, we need different activities to relieve stress in different situations.

Just as stress is different; success is different. Success is not a one-size-fits-all. What works best for one person may not work at all for another. And, what worked in the past for one or two situations may not work in future situations. Finding balance, and actively managing your time and commitments lessens stress. Our efforts will show incremental progress with practice, like marathon training. Without practice, we know that we will have health problems as well as continuing to deal with the same issues, never achieving success.

Beyond our ability or inability to function, too much stress shortens our lives just as too little stress makes our life difficult to live. Focusing on the negative side of things always increases stress; focusing only on the positive often creates problems. Balance is imperative between both positive and negative, just like the forces we evaluate when making decisions.

MEDITATION

Stress takes a toll on our bodies, our minds, and our soul. Eating well, sleeping 7-8 hours a night, regular exercise, time management, and basic socialization help lessen stress. Another tool that lessens stress is Meditation. Meditation decreases blood pressure and heart rate, while increasing gray matter or memory capacity in the brain. Even just 11 to 15 minutes of meditation can change your mood during the day and your sleep at night within a few days. It works before you go to work, bed, or both. And if you wake up during the night it helps you go back to sleep. Hundreds of thoughts flood our brains every minute. Repeating an affirmation or mantra keeps us focused and negativity from gripping our attention. Affirmations include sayings such as:

- *I focused on my Life's mission today.*

- *I was the best me today possible.*

- *I see others as gifts.*

- *I have a plan to serve others and God.*

- *I am ten times bolder today than yesterday and am taking action.*

- *I manage my life from inside out.*

- *I am destined to succeed.*

- *I let it go and relax.*

Simple mantras such as Ong, Om, Sat Nam, or Sa Ta Na Ma while sitting in a chair with a straight back or sitting on the floor helps to destress. Repeating an affirmation and/or mantra for 11 to 15 minutes, allows your blood pressure to change, your circulation to improve, your breathing to deepen, and your glands to begin emitting hormones to lower stress!

If you have time, the longer you meditate, the more changes occur in your body; at 22 minutes your brain begins to make new, connections linking your right and left brains; at 31 minutes your glands, lungs, blood pressure, and mind sync together decreasing stress and increasing memory, and at 62 minutes your Cortex thickens. When your cortex thickens, you are more able to deal with stress, have a better memory, and have more protection against Alzheimer's and other forms of dementia in old age. As with exercise, you get more benefits from being consistent. In other words, 11 minutes of meditation six days a week is **BETTER** for your sleep and memory than 62 minutes of meditation one day a week.

Stress changes like the weather. Stress unmanaged causes bad decisions and raises fear. So, creating a balance is imperative. Time management 24/7 helps. Consistently using a decision-making process improves decisions, and lessens stress. Understanding your overall mission, objectives, goals, and the tasks to achieve is required. **Stress, wisely managed, contributes to your success; unwisely managed, stress weakens your mind, memory, body, and soul!**

References

Boyles, S. (2011). Zeidan demonstrates Brain Imaging Shows Impact of Brief Mindfulness Meditation Training. Retrieved October 30, 2011 from: http://www.webmd.com/balance/news/20110406/meditation-may-reduce-pain

Dawn of a new Sleep Drug? (July 19, 2011). Retrieved from: http://online.wsj.com/article/SB1000142405 27023045676045764102061138630.html

Good, E. (1999). Venting Your Anger May Be a Bad Idea / It can increases violent behavior, researchers find. Retrieved from: http://www.sfgate.com/news/article/Venting-Your-Anger-May-Be-a-Bad-Idea-It-can-2943158.php#ixzz2Lg0puPb8

Haijtema, D. (2011). Management as meditation. Ode Magazine, Retrieved October 30, 2011 from: http://www.odemagazine.com/doc/74/management-as-meditation/

Heinrich, L., Shoham, D., Dugas, L., Kittle, N., Kurtz, A., Lees, B., Rent, S., Richie, W., Stoltenberg, M., Teng, S., Walsh, J., Weaver, M. & Wusu, M. (2011). Religious activity does not lower blood pressure. Retrieved October 30, 2011 from: http://www.loyolamedicine.org/News/News_Releases/news_release_detail.cfm?var_news_release_id=973441444

Rattana, G. (2003). Shabad Kriya: Bedtime Meditation. Retrieved on October 30, 2011 from: http://www.kundaliniyoga.org/kyt16.html

Will drinking warm milk make you sleepy. (2013). Retrieved from: http://www.uamshealth.com/?id=6752&sid=1

About Katrina

Katrina grew up in LA and earned her Bachelor's at Stephens, her Masters at University of Missouri, and is ABD at Walden University. Specializing in conflict resolution/mediation, qualitative and quantitative research, systems theory, organizational behavior, project management, competitive intelligence, and decision sciences she's worked in China, Hong Kong, Malaysia, Vietnam, and the US – training and conducting product research, product/service development and marketing. Past projects include Sprint's DSL, Talking Call Waiting, P&G Floor Care, American Express's Leadership Development.

Katrina is an author, artist/weaver, 180-year old family farm manager, Certified Project Manager, Indexer, and Mediator. Her avocations include social entrepreneurship, knitting, photography, woodcarving, and helping with genealogical research for DAC.

Katrina's presentations include: *Using Robert's Rules of Order, Native American Justice, Mark Twain, Missouri Indians, Olive VanBibber Boone, Thomas Paine and Common Sense, Truman's Politics and Economics, For the 21st Century, Stress and Safety at Home and in the Workplace, Becoming your Own Unsinkable Molly Brown, Jamestowne Spies, Online Mediation methods, techniques and training,* to name a few. Katrina volunteers in the Civil Air Patrol and racewalks competitively; she is a KCBS Barbeque Judge, Registered Yoga Teacher (RYT) in Hatha and Kundalini yoga; she is certified in Chow Qigong Medical Therapy, Reiki, Pilates, Zumba, and Yoga in Chairs for MS. She conducts research in project management and productivity, Integrative Medicine areas combining yoga, Qigong, pilates, and meditation to increase productivity and memory, help sleep and lessen stress. She is a regular columnist for Yang Sheng, a bilingual magazine/journal for healthcare professionals or preventive medicine and practitioners of mind-body exercise.

To learn more about Katrina, product development, project management, mediation, productivity and sleep, and ongoing research in Yoga for MS or Qigong Medical projects, as well as innovative ideas and *thinking outside the box*, email her at: KatrinaEverhart@yahoo.com or call 573-234-6222.

CHAPTER 15

THE MAGIC OF THE WORLD AND HOW TO MAKE THE IMPOSSIBLE POSSIBLE

BY MARCEL MARVEL

Over several years I was travelling around the world to learn from the best of the best in different areas to get a deeper understanding on visible and hidden structures and dynamics

- on how the world works and
- to find out how the human and it's subconsciousness works

by diving into a deeper reality: the "magic" in our world.

I experienced

- How to be Successful in Business and Life
- Personal Development
- Spiritual Development
- Magic and Stage Shows

Once on my journey, I had a life changing experience.

We had been a small circle of well-selected people. Our trainer taught us a special trance technique to change our state of consciousness to establish a direct line to our subconsciousness.

After this experience, I knew exactly what I wanted:

I wanted to be a Trainer, Coach and Magician.

This also led me to a problem: I knew what I wanted. But I didn't know how to achieve it. Either I'd decide to follow my dreams and passions, or I'd follow the pathway to earn money for living.

How would you have decided?

I was looking for a solution. And, finally - what did I do?

1. I GOT CLEAR ABOUT MY PRIORITIES.

For me, it was more important to follow my dreams than earn money - AND - I needed money to survive. So, how could I solve it?

2. I CHANGED MY APPROACH!

I changed the question from:

"Should I follow my dreams and passions or should I
earn money for living?"

to

"How can I earn money by following my dreams and passions?"

The question itself contains the answer that I teach to my success students.

To ask the right question can be a very powerful tool!

Have you ever been in a situation where you thought, you can't get out of this situation - and - no matter how you decide, it will be the wrong decision?

For this kind of situation, you can simply change the closed question (yes/no) into an open question (how?).

3. HAVING THE RIGHT MINDSET ALWAYS HELPS!

Good mindsets are:

"There is always at least one solution"

and the

Marcel Marvel Option Mindset:

"If you don't see a solution, it doesn't mean there isn't one."

With this mindset, I found solutions to situations where even experts in various fields told me: "There is no way!"

That's one reason why people are saying: "He makes the impossible possible."

With this mindset - You have a powerful tool! It's up to you if you use it.

7 STEPS OF PREPARATION TO BECOME A BETTER DECISION MAKER

To make it short: The more clarity and preparation you have, the better prepared you are for decision-making.

1. What do You Really Want in Life?

A good basic preparation to make good decisions is to be aware of what it is you really want in your life and visualize it. To know this for your different areas of life and business helps you align your subconscious decisions and filters and helps you make decisions faster, better and easier.

2. Hierarchy of Criteria

"Criteria" refers to the values or standards a person uses to make decisions and judgments. Values are criteria on the level of beliefs.

The hierarchy of criteria is a ranking on your personal criteria, where you know which criteria is more important to you.

A simple hierarchy of criteria could be:

1. My loved one

2. My life

3. Money

We all have our hierarchy of criteria, and we have different ones. So for one person, money is very important and for another person, health is more important.

Real vs. Illusion Hierarchy:

1. The "Illusion Hierarchy of Criteria" is the hierarchy we think we have.

2. The "Real Hierarchy of Criteria" is the hierarchy we do really have.

Quite often people are not aware about what really matters to them in which priority.

The Illusion Hierarchy of Criteria was established by our surroundings and people who influenced us everyday (like parents, teachers, friends, commercials and co-workers).

Having the inner conflict between mentally preferring one criteria and subconsciously prioritizing another one can make decisions difficult.

Keep in mind that the hierarchy of criteria can change over time and in different situations.

3. Mindset and Beliefs

Good decision mindsets are:

1. "Yippee, I can make a decision"

2. "I love to take decisions"

3. "I am a great decision maker"

4. "Making good decisions is easy to me"

5. "I'm glad to have the power to decide"

6. Any beliefs that help you make better decisions

The habit of always having to have the perfect decision isn't always the best habit.

A good approximate rule to use here is the Pareto principle: Invest 10% effort with 90% outcome (alternatively 20% effort, 80% outcome). It depends on the situation. In most cases it's not worth investing 80% effort for the last 20% percent of outcome.

Making decisions and taking action is a very important habit to take control over your life. Not taking decisions equals giving away responsibility. Giving away responsibility equals to waiving your power - your power over your life!

Remember: You are always responsible for the decisions you take. And you are responsible for your decisions you don't take.

Taking no decision is a decision too!

4. The Boundary

Get clear about the borders and boundaries inside which you will act.

Examples:
- Never ever should anyone die by my actions and decisions.
- Only work together with honest people.

5. Get Rid of the Fear

The fear of loss holds back a lot of people from making decisions. If they'd make a decision, they'd lose all the other options.

The worry about "what if it was the wrong decision" can make people change their decision many times back and forth.

To be a good decision-maker, you have to overcome this fear.

There are several tools out there to overcome decision-making fears. For example, you can combine EFT (Emotional Freedom Technique) by Gary Craig and practice decision-making.

Don't overlook the benefit of fear and perfectionism. Decide for yourself what's the best amount of perfectionism and fear for you to support your decisions.

6. Prepare Decisions for Frequent and Important Situations

The idea is to be prepared in these situations to decide quicker, better and easier. It is very helpful for recurring situations as well as other situations for which you want to be prepared.

a. Make a list with decision situations you will be confronted with.

b. Select those for which you want to be prepared.

c. Prepare strategies for those situations (i.e. preselect decision method).

7. Habit: Be in a Good State of Mind and Take Action

Make it a habit being comfortable to take good, quick decisions.

This is something you can learn and train to do. Just do it! The more you practice, the easier it will be. The most difficult part is when you start.

As always: The right mindset helps!

If you take a decision, it helps to be in a good decision-making state. You can prepare for this by a good lifestyle (i.e. health, sports, nutrition, fun, energy...).

Successful people tend to stay within the decision they made and only change it if there is really a reason - and - only after carefully thinking about it.

It usually helps to be relaxed and focused while making a decision.

Again, making decisions and taking action are very important habits to have control over your life!

Usually it's better to take a decision than not taking one. Even to outsource specific decisions to an expert or consult an expert can be a helpful decision.

7 STEPS TO MAKE BETTER DECISIONS

As mentioned above, it's always good to be prepared for decision-making. It depends on the situation if it's better to make a quick decision.

1. Define the Problem

First define the problem to give you clarity about the problem. The goal is to express the issue in a clear, one-sentence problem statement that describes both, the initial conditions and the desired conditions.

2. Determine the Requirements

In the second step, you define the conditions that any acceptable solution of the problem must meet. It describes what the solution must do to the problem (i.e., ROI-Factor of at least 1.5).

3. Establish Goals that Solving the Problem Should Accomplish

It's difficult to take a decision without knowing what you want to achieve. Thus question yourself with a clear goal in mind.

The goals you define here go beyond the minimum requirements. Be sure to set the right goals and set them in the right manner. Details on good and correct goal-setting is described in my other materials and training.

Example: State the goals positively and avoid negations like "not."

Decision-making is easier if you are clear about what you want and are aware of your hierarchy of criteria.

4. Identify Options That will Solve the Problem

By evaluating the requirements and goals, you can work out options and alternatives. The more options you have, the more opportunities you have and the more complex the decision is. Only consider options that meet the requirements and screen out options which don't.

5. Develop the Criteria Based on the Goals

Here you define the decision criteria, which will discriminate among alternatives. They must be based on the goals. They are objective measures of the goals how well each option achieves the goals.

6. Select the Decision Making Tool and Apply it to Select the Preferred Option

There are several decision-making tools out there. Choose the best decision-making tool for your decision. As in the preparation section mentioned above, it helps if you have predefined which decision tool is useful with what kind of decision.

Taking decisions is usually eliminating a variety of options to come down to one option, the one option of your choice. Finally, decision-making is focusing on the option you decide. The best decision strategy depends on the situation, the context and yourself.

It depends on the situation if you should listen more to your heart, your mind or your stomach, or bring them into alignment. Generally, it's a good sign if your heart, stomach and your mind agree on a decision.

A good check in love relationships: Do you and your partner match at the levels of mind, heart and sexuality. If there is one non-matching area, it's a "signal" to check what's up there and then decide what to do or just accept it.

Keep in mind that your subconscious mind can process more information than your conscious mind. Being able to listen to your subconscious mind can help you make good decisions faster.

7. Check the Answer to make Sure it Solves the Problem

Finally, it's a good idea to check if your answer solves the problem. If it does not, you did something wrong earlier. If it solves the problem you are done with the seven steps. Congratulations!

7 STEPS TO ELICIT YOUR HIERARCHY OF CRITERIA

(For more detailed information, please visit: www.magic-success.com)

1. Brainstorm on Values and Criteria

First of all, collect your criteria using a brainstorm technique you like and that work for you best.

This step's rule: The more - the better.

2. Eliminate Criteria not Important to You

Now - after you get your collection of criteria - eliminate the criteria not important to you and select the important ones to you.

More criteria will lead into more work and better results. Less criteria will lead into less work and poorer results.

You can save all your criteria for future use (even the unimportant ones).

3. Number Consecutively

List the criteria numerically:

Example:
1. My loved one
2. Money
3. My life

There is no specific order. Just give each criterion a random number.

4. Compare Criteria with Each Other

Compare criteria with one another and define which is more important to you. So you compare:

Compare		Result
1	2	1
1	3	1
2	3	3
...	...	...

The result in the first row (1, 2; 1) describes that criterion #1 is more important than criterion #2 by comparing criteria #1 and #2.

As you can see in the third row (2, 3; 3) the result shows that criterion #3 is more important than criterion #2 by comparing criteria #2 and #3.

5. Count the Winner

Now you count how many times each criteria is more important than the other one.

Our Example:

Nr.	Criteria	Count
1	My loved one	2
2	Money	0
3	My life	1

You see, you got criterion #1 the most times, followed by criterion #3 and finally criterion #2.

6. Sort Winner

Simply sort the results by the count. The criterion with the highest count wins. It is the most important of the criteria!

Our Example:

Rank	Nr.	Criteria	Count
1	1	My loved one	2
2	3	My life	1
3	2	Money	0

7. Check the Hierarchy

The final step is to check if the hierarchy is correct. Just compare each criterion with its following criteria. If you did everything right, the hierarchy should be correct.

If you find something wrong, then you probably made a mistake before. Just update the hierarchy until you have the correct one.

SUGGESTIONS ON THE HIERARCHY OF CRITERIA?

1. It is absolute important to know your top 3 Values!

2. Usually it's a good idea to know about 7 +/-2 values (5-9), because this is the amount of chunks (=information pieces) most people process at a time. Try out what works best for you.

3. Recognize and check out the number of criteria you feel comfortable with.

4. Learn them so that you can access them immediately – even if I wake you up out of a deep sleep.

5. After a while you can check your hierarchy of criteria again and check out if and how it changes.

DECISION MAKING METHODS

10-10-10 Method

One simple method (from S. Welch) to make decisions is asking yourself the following questions:

What effects will my decision have in 10 days?

What effects will my decision have in 10 months?

What effects will my decision have in 10 years?

This gives you another perspective on your decision.

Energy Decision

Another good way is to see the decision from the view of energy:

How much energy does it give me?

How much energy does it cost me?

You can perceive energy as a kind of metaphor (including physical and mental energy, money value energy, stress factor, love ...). If you don't like the word energy, just substitute it with what you are comfortable.

About Marcel

Born as Marcel Fleisch, also known as "The Man Who Makes the Impossible Possible," he travelled around the world for 16 years. His philosophy: "Learn the Best from the Best of the Best."

Marcel Marvel enjoyed meeting experts, masters, elders and superstars of different cultures and knowledge to learn from, and experience with them.

On his "hero's journey," Marcel Marvel experienced long-held secrets, discovered apparently lost knowledge and discovered what makes the most successful people different from others.

Marcel Marvel found over generations long-held secret knowledge and experiences. Based on his experiences and deep findings, Marcel Marvel developed the Magic Success® System.

As a magician, Marcel Marvel toured successfully in many countries all over the world and people loved to see him in Las Vegas and Hollywood.

After successfully finishing his education at the Commercial Academy in Austria, Marcel Marvel studied computer science at the Vienna University of Technology and finished as a certified degreed engineer with a Master's degree in Science. Marcel Marvel graduated as "Diplom Mental Trainer" and, after several years of governmental education, he graduated to become a registered mediator at the Government's Department of Justice in Austria.

Now he combines his skills as:

- A highly-skilled success expert and trainer
- University certified trainer and consultant
- Professional magician (Alumni of Magic and Mystery School – Las Vegas)

to mold him into the Magic Success® Trainer & Coach.

By melding together the knowledge and experience collected worldwide over 16 years, Marcel Marvel developed a completely new and unique method, which takes people faster and easier to their goals.

By fusing together new technology, old secrets and forgotten wisdom, success strategies from various areas of knowledge by experts, masters, elders and superstars from around the world – Marcel Marvel developed the powerful and very unique Magic Success® System.

Marcel Marvel's strategies and systems create completely new dimensions and opportunities, methods and finally new chances.

As Magic Success® Trainer and Coach, he helps corporations and individuals to achieve their goals and make their dreams come true.

To find out more about **Marcel Marvel, Magic Success®, Success, Decisions, Trainings, Shows, Coaching and Consulting** visit his website and follow him at Facebook, Twitter, LinkedIn or Xing.

Website: http://www.magic-success.com

Twitter: http://www.twitter.com/MarcelMarvel1

CHAPTER 16

ENTREPRENEURSHIP

BY PATRICIA HUDON

What is it? According to the dictionary, entrepreneurship is the state, quality, or condition of being an entrepreneur, an organizer, promoter of business ventures, or the duration of a person's function as an entrepreneur. An entrepreneur is a person who organizes, operates, and assumes the risk of a business venture. (Free Dictionary, 2013.)

ON THE WAY TO BEING AN ENTREPRENEUR

There comes a time in everyone's life when they need to move on to bigger and better things, so after spending 24 years in the Air Force and 11 ½ years as an auditor for the Federal Government, it came my time to retire. Retirement means many things to many people – for me it meant moving back to my childhood home place and building the home of my dreams – a log house in the woods. In August 2005, Hurricane Katrina provided the logs that would eventually become part of that dream because big beautiful pines do not hold up well to such a powerful force. When it was over, they lay all over my cousin's yard in south Louisiana like pickup sticks, crisscross and on top of each other, what a mess. There were so many trees around his house that no one except those that came to visit him knew a house was there until Katrina came through and wiped out 90 percent of the trees, which miraculously, not one hit the house.

Instead of letting all those trees go to waste he drove to Columbia, Missouri, bought a portable band sawmill and cut a log house package that sat in storage curing so someone could build it – not knowing that someone was going to be me. At the time I lived in Kansas City, Missouri, with no intentions of retiring any time soon as I had a good paying job as an Auditor for the Federal Government. Let 5 years go by and in October 2010, I met him and his brother at the Ozark Music Festival in Mountain View, Arkansas for a few days of fun listening to the old time music – while there he asked if I was ever going to move home since I had been gone for well over 35 years. I said I had thought about it but had no plans at that time. The log house package came up during that conversation, so I asked if he was interested in selling it. Hence, my house was started in March 2011, and I decided to retire for a second time in December that same year and move south where it was warmer so I could work from home. I also had a part-time job teaching college on-line and my intentions were to teach full time. Instead, I decided to reopen a business I had started and closed during my first retirement, only this time I was going to do things a bit differently.

Four things I am doing differently this time around. Several are already in place and several are in the plans.

1. I am not doing all the work, I took my business on-line and found drop shippers to process the orders and ship the gift baskets rather than make and deliver them all myself. Setting a business up that way limits how far you can go and you eventually burn out, which I did and closed it because I simply could not keep up. However, with drop shipping, all I need to do is market the baskets, take the orders, and forward them to the drop shipper – who in turn makes the gift basket and delivers it to the customer with all of my information, just as if I had made it myself.

2. I am setting up a constant content stream. No matter what the business, online or brick and mortar, creating content online is a great way to promote a business and generate leads. I have created a website, a blog, and have a presence on Facebook, Pinterest, and Twitter in an effort to get my business out there and seen.

3. I plan to find a better balance between creating content myself and having guest-help create and promote both businesses – mine and theirs. There is great value in balancing my content

with others that have a similar passion as we each have something unique to offer due to our experiences and expertise and that gives more depth and variety to the content. You also get the added benefit of a connection with other experts, which may lead to joint ventures, partnerships, referral relationships, and promotion of your venture.

4. I would have worried more about passion than profit – if you have passion and it shows, then the money will eventually flow. Once you are connected to a bigger purpose in life and business, things will start to fall into place and synchronize. (Riviere, 2010.)

STARTING A HOME-BASED BUSINESS

There are many reasons to start your own home-based business. However, the most popular is preference to work for yourself, be your own boss, and make the decisions. To be successful as a business owner, you must possess the same skills that successful employees possess and be willing to work long, hard hours to make the business profitable. It also helps if your business has products or services consumers need and want.

Unfortunately, for various reasons about 70 percent of small-businesses fail within the first 5 years. Typical reasons include undercapitalization (lack of enough money), poor location, poor customer service, unqualified or untrained employees, fraud, lack of a proper business plan, and/or failure to seek professional help. (Pride, Hughes, & Kapoor, 2008.)

HOME BUSINESS 'MUSTS'

There are certain 'musts' that are required to be successful in any endeavor you pursue. Whether it is driving a car, playing sports, or retiring comfortably, your goal is to be successful. Therefore if you are to be successful in business, your formula should be no different – there are certain 'musts' that have to be fully developed, implemented, and managed for your business to succeed. Although there are many 'musts', I will present 25 that I think are important to start, operate, and grow a successful, profitable home-based business:

1. Do what you enjoy – have a passion for what you do. If you do

not enjoy the business, chances are it will fail. What you put into your business is what you will get out of it.

2. Take what you do seriously – if you expect to be successful you must truly believe in your business and what it has to offer customers (i.e., goods and services). To be successful you must "keep your nose to the grindstone" and not let yourself get sidetracked or unmotivated. Don't fall prey to the naysayers that do not take you seriously and think you really do not have a job simply because you work from home. Set boundaries for visits during your office hours – since they do not think you have a job they think you have all the time in the world to visit or do other things. What I hear most is, "Well you are home all day, why can't you do that." It is because I have a job.

3. Plan everything – This is a must as it builds habits every business owner should develop, implement, and maintain – it requires you to analyze each business situation, research and compile data, and make conclusions based on facts revealed through research. It also puts your goals and how you plan to achieve them on paper creating a road map to take you from point A to point Z.

4. Manage your money wisely – Money is the lifeblood of any business, you must buy inventory, or other things such as services you need, promote and market your business, repair or replace tools and equipment, and if you plan to survive, pay yourself so you do not have to go out and find another job working for someone else. Therefore, all home-based business owners must become wise money managers to ensure the cash keeps flowing (income) and the bills get paid (expenses).

5. Ask for the sale – There is no better way to get a sale than to simply ask for it. All the marketing, advertising, or promotional activities are for naught –regardless of how clever, expensive, or perfectly targeted – unless you do one simple thing…ask for the sale!

6. Remember it is all about the customer – Your business is all about the customer or client, not the products or services you sell, the prices you charge, or even your competition and how to beat them, it is simply about the customer or client. Without

customers you will not have a business, therefore everything you do must be customer-oriented. Your policies, warranties, payment options, operating hours, presentations, advertising and promotional campaigns and website must be customer-focused and you must know your customers inside out.

7. Become a shameless self-promoter (without becoming obnoxious) – This is one of the most beneficial, yet most underutilized, marketing tools you have at your disposal. Do it wisely and you can get your name, products, and services out there for customers to see.

8. Project a positive business image – You must always go out of your way to make a positive business image, remember first impressions are lasting impressions and all you have is but a passing moment to make a positive and memorable impression on people you intend to do business with.

9. Get to know your customers – One advantage small home-based businesses have over larger competitors – they can personalize their attention by answering the phones and getting to know customers which create repeat business and according to research about 80% of business is repeat customers.

10. Level the playing field with technology – Simply put, make sure you have a favorable presence on the Internet. The best technology is that which helps you in your business – therefore you should know how to take advantage of using it.

11. Build a top-notch business team – Remember you cannot do it alone. It is a task that requires a team committed to you and your business and its success. Also remember that your customers and clients are part of that team and any or all will have a say in how your business will function and its future.

12. Become known as an expert – The more you become known for your expertise, the more people will seek you out, creating more selling and referral opportunities. This is known as reverse prospecting since people will seek you out for your expertise rather than you having to find new customers to sell to.

13. Create a competitive advantage – You must answer one of two questions, "Why will people choose to do business with me instead of doing business with my competitor?" or "What separates my business from my competition?" Maybe it is better service, a longer warranty, better selection, better customer service, or many other reasons – whatever it is, it must set you apart.

14. Invest in yourself – Become an avid reader of business and marketing materials (books, magazines, articles, reports, journals, newsletters, websites, and industry publications) to improve your understanding of business and marketing skills and functions. Join business associations and clubs, network with other skilled business people to learn secrets of their success to help define your goals and objectives. Attend business and marketing seminars, workshops and training courses because education is an ongoing process. In other words become a life-long learner of your business to stay on top.

15. Be accessible – Be cognizant of the fact that few people will go out of their way, or be inconvenienced just for the privilege of giving you their money – you must make it as easy as you can. Making it easy means being accessible and knowledgeable about your products and services.

16. Build a rock-solid reputation – This is unquestionably one of your most tangible and marketing assets – you cannot buy a good reputation, you must earn it. If you make promises, keep them, and be consistent in what you offer on a regular basis otherwise they have no reason to trust you...without trust, you will not have a good reputation.

17. Sell Benefits – What are the benefits of owning your product or using your services? Your advertising, sales presentations, printed marketing materials, product packaging, website, newsletters, or any other medium used should communicate to your audience the benefits associated with owning your products or using your services.

18. Get involved – Community involvement such as local charities or organizing community events, even getting involved in local politics are a must for the success of your business. People like to do business with someone they know, respect, and like, and help the community to grow.

19. Grab attention – Promotional activity must put money back in your pocket so you can continue to grow your business and grab more attention.

20. Master the art of negotiations – This is one skill you must make every effort to master, second only to simply asking for the sale, as negotiations skills are used on a daily basis. Your negotiation skills should always orchestrate a win-win situation, which means everyone involved feels they have won – thereby building long-term and profitable business relationships.

21. Design your workspace for success – If at all possible have a separate room with a door, if that is not possible then find a means of converting a room with a partition or simply find hours to do the bulk of your work when no one else is at home. Carefully plan and design your workspace to ensure maximum personal performance and productivity.

22. Get and stay organized – getting organized is about managing your business and having systems in place to get things done, not so much about having a few stacks of paper on your desk. Therefore you want to establish a routine by which you can accomplish as much as possible in any given workday. Simple things like creating a to-do list at the end of each day will help keep you on top of important tasks to tackle.

23. Take time off – Create a regular work schedule that includes breaks, days off, and even vacations, so you do not become burned out. Understand also that you must maintain some flexibility.

24. Limit the number of hats you wear – Learn what you are good at and what you should delegate to others. You simply cannot do it all.

25. Follow-up constantly – This should be the mantra of every home business owner since it enables you to turn prospects into customers, increasing the value of each sale. It also increases the buying frequency from existing customers and builds stronger relationships with suppliers and your core business team.

Building a business takes hard work and dedication therefore it is best you do something you like and have a passion for. In all likelihood, it is safe to assume that your passion will reflect in the success of your business (Stephenson, n.d.).

References

The Free Dictionary, (2013), retrieved February 15, 2013, from: http://www.thefreedictionary.com/entrepreneurship

Pride, William M., Hughes, Robert J., & Kapoor, J., Business, (2008), Chapter 1, *Exploring the World of Business and Economics*, South-Western Centage Learning, Mason, OH 45040

Riviere, Amber (2010), Do-Overs: *5 Things I would do differently in Business,* retrieved February 15, 2013: http://gigaom.com/2010/06/03/do-overs-5-things-i-would-do-differently-in-business/

Stephenson, James, (n.d.), *25 Common characteristics of Successful Entrepreneurs*, retrieved February 17, 2013 from: http://www.entrepreneur.com/article/200730

About Patricia

Patricia A. Hudon

Grantham University, Southern New Hampshire University, and Virginia College Online.

Patricia Hudon, (MA, Webster University), is an Adjunct Professor of Business, Accounting, and Human Resources at Grantham University, an Adjunct Professor of Human Resources at Southern New Hampshire University, and an Adjunct Professor of Accounting at Virginia College Online. Professor Hudon was awarded the Faculty of the Year Award in 2010 at Grantham University. She is retired from the Air Force with 24 years of service and worked for the Department of Veterans Affairs as a Senior Auditor for 11½ years before retiring in December 2011. Professor Hudon has been an adjunct professor since December 2007. She is a member of the Association of Government Accountants and a life member of the Air Force Sergeant's Association.

Patricia started her home-based business PH Distributing, LLC, aka: Patti's Baskets and Gifts, in July 2012. To learn more and receive her monthly newsletter, visit: www. pattisbasketsandgifts.com.

CHAPTER 17

A REFLECTIVE LOOK AT COMMITTING TO SUCCESS

BY LAURA CLANCY

OBJECTIVES OF THIS CHAPTER:

By the end of this chapter, you should be able to determine the following: When is it too late to achieve long term success?

Once Upon A Time, as all good (success) stories begin...

...there lived a youngster named Pat. Pat came from a family with a mama, papa and baby sib. As life whizzed by, Pat grew physically and emotionally through each experience lived.

One day as Pat was outside playing, a bright and shiny object magically appeared on the ground beside him. Overcome with curiosity, he picked it up. This special obsidian was not something indigenous to Pat's world and he was unaware of its origin.

Pat reflected upon what was staring back from the shiny object. It was another child who appeared to be the same age as the now ashen Pat! What was going on? Who was *THAT* on the opposite side of shiny? How could someone, who appeared to move only when Pat moved, live in FLAT?

Suddenly, a 'dirty thunderstorm' erupted and Pat dropped the shiny object like a molten-hot potato and scurried home. Enough scary stuff for one day! If Pat had remained long enough, or held onto the stone, he would have witnessed a polished life, quite the opposite of his own, unfolding.

From that day forward, what Pat experienced from the senses of sight, sound, smell, taste and touch created feelings based on emotion. These feelings became so strong and ingrained that they influenced Pat's actions in daily activities. You see, Pat became a product of bad programming... where emotionally-driven decisions and fears outweigh logic and faith in oneself.

As Pat grew into adulthood, more and more of those emotionally charged decisions wholly affected his life's results and his failures were compounded. Pat lived as if embedded in a lava flow, passively following the path of least resistance and destroying his surroundings as he went.

For example, Pat was a dormant student in college. Graduating at the bottom of his class, Pat had limited choices for employment. Once out in the wide world of commerce, Pat discovered a new universe, an exciting world that so obviously had opportunities and was full of abundance. Pat desperately wanted to pursue those opportunities and have a blast.

Alas! Success was elusive. Each opportunity pursued led to repeated failure. Life was a complex volcano and Pat appeared to be at fault. It seemed that success was something Pat could never tap into.

Meanwhile, back in the land of FLAT, Pat's reflection brought life-flow from extinction. From the moment that Pat dropped the shiny object, a fissured character was born. Tap, the mirror twin of Pat, was created.

In Tap's world, life unfolded in daily wonderment. Each day Tap's five senses were awakened in such a way that no feat seemed out of reach. Each negative situation was resolved with lessons learned and each positive scenario unfolded with blessings counted.

Tap found FLATLAND "U" challenging, but made straight "A's" a priority. Upon his graduation, employment opportunities abounded. Many companies could see that Tap's work ethic and perseverance would be an asset to their company's success. Tap made choices wisely. Fear, when it crept in, was kept at bay and calculated decisions were made to reach monumental goals. Tap was a landslide success in every avenue of life. Tap scaled every mountain and found success at each ridge.

Though it seems that we reach THE END with a clear "winner" and "loser," this story doesn't end because infinite possibilities still remain. You see, in the real world, the potential for long term success is endless, no matter who or where you are in life.

Though it appeared that success was something Pat could never tap into, *THAT* wasn't the mirror image's 'plane' truth. After many setbacks and roadblocks, Pat decided to take a thoughtful and difficult look at reality; he journeyed into self-awareness. Pat made a leap of faith to change the results created by his bad daily decisions and took to heart the anonymous quote, "In order to get something you never had, you have to do things you have never done."

Pat did the one thing that was absolutely imperative to changing insufficient results: Pat *COMMITTED* to change.

In the controlled environment of FLAT, that was the advantage Tap had over Pat...but, not for long...Pat was now taking the driver's seat and refused to fall asleep at the wheel or even move forward with cruise control. You see, in the past, Pat **wanted** change (a superficial and useless level of desire for long-term success), and sometimes even **chose** change (a level of desire that allows fleeting success.)

Now, it was time to **commit** to change. This one change set Pat up to achieve success, no matter what.

Along the journey of commitment, two things happened: Pat became 1) self-aware and 2) used the tool of faking it 'til making it. Pat realized that change on the outside would only be possible by change on the inside. Pat decided to take a controlled, logical approach to decision making, allowing logic to outwit negative emotional programming formed long ago. Pat also feigned success until the illusion of success became a metamorphic reality.

In the end, Pat *flat out* earned and achieved more success than Tap because overcoming (emotional) obstacles made him even stronger than his hard-working twin.

And the moral is: **No matter how many times you've been defeated, it's never too late to achieve long term success.**

Is this a made up story? Of course it is! But how cool would it be...

... to have a mirror twin who made bad decisions and had different outcomes from the other twin? Yet, eventually through self-awareness and committed change, wound up in nearly the same place at the end of the story? One twin would just have a few more of life's battle scars, giving him a competitive edge.

Is it a story that's somewhat reflective of my life? You bet!

Before I became a six-time world record holding powerlifter and best-selling author, I was Laura Clancy, the overweight bean counter and full time stay-at-home mom.

How did I get from "there" to "here"? I'll tell you, but only after 'drilling down to bedrock.'

For some, success appears to come naturally from birth. Perhaps they were born with a "competitive advantage of money." They're considered to have a "silver spoon" in their mouth and success seems within easy reach. For others, it appears that success is gained on a daily basis, even against many odds.

I subscribe to the theory that everyone who's successful has earned it. Nobody gets far in life based on the metallic composition of the utensil protruding from their orifice. This means that ANYONE can earn success...and when YOU achieve that success, you can show others how to follow suit; leading by example.

In the fitness field, we know that long term bad habits leading to clients physical ailments can be reversed and nearly erased with a daily regimen of good nutrition and exercise. This philosophy holds true with the quest for any success. Bad results from years of constant misadventures can erode, and be eclipsed by, each new success achieved. Success builds momentum by stacking up and creating a tipping point toward an eternally-successful life.

How cool is *THAT*?

If there's one thing I've learned on the journey to long-term success, both mine and my clients, it's that whatever goal you set, you must *COMMIT* your entire being to achieving that goal. As I took my own journey of self-awareness many years ago, I came across the idea of Manifestation Process, which takes the theory of Law of Attraction and makes it an enforceable law. This process resonated with me.

If you aren't familiar with this particular line of thinking, the quick and dirty version is that: thoughts become feelings become actions become results. That meant that my prior lack of success wasn't a problem, it was a result. Duh, right?

Going deeper, I learned that my past *programming* became thoughts became actions became results. What's programming? Programming is how your mind perceives reality. Like a computer, your brain's taken everything it's heard, seen and experienced since you were a baby and processed it. In turn, processing produced thoughts and feelings that have become how you think and feel about EVERYTHING. Our responses to weight, food, exercise, money, politics, religion and every other aspect of our lives comes from early experiences and conditioning, our programming. Boiled down to basics, your programming is your subconscious mind.

Why is that important? Because in an epic battle between "logic" and "emotion", EMOTION will almost always win. Logically, you want to be successful...but, emotionally, you may not be ready for it. It's worth a pause here to think about how you feel about "success" or "successful people". It's important for you to know how you feel about this subject because it could be your first step toward self-awareness.

Let's assume that you have some type of negative feeling toward success or successful people. Does that surprise you? I had a negative perception of successful people and it surprised me. As much as I admired the successful people I knew, I was afraid to be one of them. One of my biggest obstacles in the success equation was that I was afraid to commit to success creation and doing what it took to remain successful. I mean, really, how long can you smile for the camera? In addition, I viewed successful people as having the "it" factor. Since I had the dreadful impostor complex, I didn't think I matched up to "them." I was afraid that I wasn't good enough to be successful or that I might change on the inside and be a little more self-centered. These were just a few of my judgmental attitudes, but they were crucial ones.

Stated Succinctly: Sustainable success-driven living seemed like a sacrifice to me.

Guess what? The logic of "becoming successful" and staying in the moment, making mindful choices, was circumvented by my negative emotions of what long term successful choices would entail. Realizing that change had to come from within, I figured out that unless I interceded and revised my way of thinking/being, I would not achieve long term success.

Let's move onto that second change that commitment fated me to make: I "faked" it 'til I "maked" it. (Yes, I know that's bad grammar, but it rhymes better.) How did I achieve success and move out of living in such a boring place once upon a time?

What? What? What could I give my clients and readers to help them achieve long term success? What was that invisible force? Was Darth Vader going to show up with a light stick and show me? (Though I sometimes live a life of delusion, Darth Vader's appearance was unlikely because hallucinations aren't one of my issues.)

Friends told me that they saw me being successful as a coach, a writer and speaker long before I knew I could be, and at first I was flummoxed. Then, I began to realize that just as I perceive those who are physically and emotionally strong as more successful, my friends saw me that way. Being a stay-at-home bean-counting mom did not drain me of the vitality that others saw.

After (im)patiently waiting for an answer to the question of how to create long-term success, it came to me: ***It took time.***

You see, I was an impostor...for a while.

What!?!

Yes, I faked success until I became it. When I graduated from college and then National Personal Training Institute, competed in my first powerlifting meet, wrote my first chapter, I would tell people, "I'm an accountant, trainer, competitive power lifter, and writer." Because I was just beginning my journey using those labels, I felt phony. But as time passed and I gained more experience, I became my labels. Now, I am not only a powerlifter and writer, I'm a WORLD-RECORD-HOLDING powerlifter and BEST-SELLING author!

At first, it all felt fake...and it made me nervous to make those statements.

But over time I was able to say those words without hesitation, because they are now part of my reality. I faked it until I not only "maked it", I became "it". Like Pat, I stumbled through years of not being successful, while the true conduit to success turned out to be choosing to commit to my own success and letting time pass.

Isn't it sensational that you can choose success with purpose by taking daily action steps? You can change your results from this moment forward when you "Commit to Success." My commitment rewarded me with success just as yours will reward you and your clients!

HERE'S YOUR SUCCESS MINDSET "TO GO" PACKAGE:

1. Commit:
Set the goal.

Commit to reach that goal.

Take daily action steps to achieve each goal.

2. Become Self-aware:
Look honestly at how you feel about anything related to success. This is a difficult step, because it's hard to be honest with yourself. However, this step reaps BIG benefits, and step 3 is practically nonsensical without this step being fully explored.

3. Reprogram negative thoughts about success:
One tool that can help you put re-programming into action, is the use of Accessions. An accession (pronounced access-shun) is a noun meaning, "a belief in the goodness of something." It reminds me of an accessory that pulls a whole outfit together. Perfect! Accessions are a valuable tool because they involve you in your own success. Stated emphatically out loud, they create a positive energy for the person stating them. I have one for you, if you care to use it: "I commit to progress my success." However, you can create any accession that's more meaningful to you. It should be stated emphatically out loud three times in a row twice a day. Three reps / Two Sets. Say it until you believe it. See it until you believe it. Experience it in your imagination until you believe it. It takes time for these accessions to become your reality, but is SO worth the effort.

4. Fake it 'til you make it:
In reality, it's often hard to tell when and where one world starts and the other ends. Our choices become pivot points where endless results can be achieved. Believe that you are who you've become the moment you achieve the goals you set. Eventually, it will be time-tested true.

Once you master your inner workings, your results will change. The successful mindset will become easier, I promise. It all begins at the root of the problem...to change those thoughts. Little tweaks can create big changes. *Programming leads to thoughts leads to actions leads to results.* Accessions lead to reprogrammed thoughts leads to beneficial actions leads to different long term results.

You will feel better. You will have success and contentment since successful people have a high degree of autonomy. Everyone desires autonomy; just ask my husband and children. Though that self-reliant independence is scary, and maybe not something that's familiar, you'll realize over time, it's the best way to live. You will win at the game of life.

As the Story of Pat and Tap show, in the looking glass of life, our successful personal grooming takes commitment and creating the illusion of success until we are able to step into the success mold we create for ourselves. Even human settlements as old as 9000 years have contained mirrors of polished **obsidian**; and self-reflection has been with us since the dawn of consciousness.

Isn't it time you mirror your own success?

The End

SUCCESS CHAPTER QUESTIONS:

Are you READY for your success mind**SET** to **GO**? In our wonderfully complex world, it's NEVER too late to achieve long term success!

About Laura

Laura Clancy is the proud owner of Muffin Toppled™ Fitness Coaching (www.muffintoppled.com) in North Arlington, Virginia. In other ventures, she's a co-author of the Best-Selling book *Results Fitness* and author and creator of WIT and FIT™, which includes the Food-Con(trol) system. She recently launched Wit and Fit's Baker's Dozen speaking engagements, a system designed to get participants whole health well.

In another life, Laura counted beans. She holds a B.S. (that's telling) in Accounting from George Mason University. Before 1999, the only weight that she had ever lifted was a fork fully loaded with sweet food. With her 20th High School Reunion looming, she began weight-lifting with a personal trainer to get to her magic weight. But when the party ended, her High School Crush receded from consciousness and the pounds came back.

Recognizing the short-lived nature of the High School Crush Diet Plan and so many others, Laura got serious and re-toppled her own muffin, leaping from amateur status to professional. By 2009, Laura had become a Certified Personal Trainer and Certified Nutrition Consultant at the National Personal Training Institute. Laura has never looked back and has plenty to share from all she's learned along the way.

In addition to training others to lift weights and conquer fat, Laura is a competitive powerlifter and at the end of 2012, held six world records. She proudly lifts with Team Force (www.teamforcepowerlifting.com). As a fitness professional living, loving, and laughing in Northern Virginia, Laura shares stories from her well-stocked humor arsenal to inspire women everywhere to get fit and eat well.

Currently, Laura trains clients of varying levels of fitness and consults on nutrition, but her real passion lies in giving seminars and workshops. She finds the most joy in helping women believe that THEY CAN DO IT TOO...if they just step into the weight-training section of the gym.

CHAPTER 18

NEW RULES OF SUCCESS FOR BALANCING WORK AND FAMILY FOR WOMEN

BY SAPPHIRE GRAY

PRELUDE AND INTRODUCTION

Dear Reader:

This chapter is a complete guide for women who are in start-up phase or currently running a business.

I want to share my personal journey with you, of being Mother, Wife and a successful Business Woman, and how I balance a busy work schedule with my personal and family commitments.

Being a teenage mum at 14 years old in the 1980's was seen as taboo, as well as being in children homes, having serious issues with men. Life was hard and there were some really depressing moments, with little support. I wanted more than just being a single parent living on government support, so I educated myself – gaining several qualifications.

Having a conventional job took away my time from my family, which was hard, so I made a decision that changed the rest of our lives...

My first business in the 90's was dressmaking and cake baking. However, I started to turn into a consultant on food and fashion. While I really enjoyed this, many of my friends started to have children young and turn to me for advice on making extra money. This intern began my new journey of helping other people with their dreams of having a business and great family life balance. With a few adjustments and the support of the family, this became the start of "Work and Life Balance for Women" – only back then I didn't know this...

The last two decades have seen a number of women choosing to work from home. A recent study of home businesses showed a growth of around 32 percent; these are generally both part-time and full-time businesses.

1. HAVING A HOME BUSINESS

Although there are many reasons why women are attracted to home enterprises, my personal experience is that I could organize my day around the family, school runs, events, and husband-time. The fact that I was also able to grow, have personal satisfaction and make my own decisions, is the best.

A home business gave me a great sense of self-determination and personal contentment. Conversely, you have to understand that to become truly successful, the level of commitment needs to be in place not only from you, but also your family members as they will be part of your business journey and growth.

2. RELATIONSHIPS
(CHILDREN/HUSBAND/BUSINESS OWNER)

(a). Children

Children are another focus when running a business. Making time for them is a crucial element to their development and your success. Allocating time wisely will not only bond the family as a unit, but will also bring you closer. I achieved this by apportioning family time within my weekly schedule.

I found that doing simple activities such as playing board games or even watching a movie showed them that although mummy had a business, I still had time for them.

Now my children are young adults with children of their own, and able to have a bigger input regarding family time. They have always been happy with our arrangements, because we were doing it together as a family.

(b). Significant other

Running a Business can be very lonely and we often turn to our significant other for reassurance and support, often forgetting that they need the same. I for one have been guilty of neglecting my husband due to my business commitments.

Cultivating your relationship should be one of your main priorities. Changing some of our working week and going back to basics, we arranged dates. Some nights we would see a movie, have candle-light dinner at home or just a glass of wine. We both felt rejuvenated, more loving, and confident; however, we never discussed work or children, as it was about us.

This also had a positive impact in our working day, as my husband was winning several awards and the business was growing, but not at the expense of our family.

(c). Me Time

Falling ill in 2005, I realised how important it was to look after my health and have frequent, "Me Time." Recharging your batteries will not only help you and your family, but will also have a positive impact on your business. Running a business and family is not easy and it takes a lot of energy, but this can be eased by a few simple steps.

Once a week I would treat myself either a glass of wine in a bubble bath with candles and music, immerse myself in a good book, an early night or a real treat would be a spa day. Staying healthy is paramount to the development of your business, so make sure you exercise and eat at regular intervals. You must give yourself a lunch break, as this will make you more productive. These things may seem simple, but we often forget to do them.

3. LIMITING BELIEFS AS THE BUSINESS OWNER

When you look in a mirror, who do you see?

Yes it's you, sometimes we forget to look at ourselves and see what others see. When I started my business, I was so focused on getting the business right for my customers and not looking at whether it was right for me and my family. People buy people, not necessarily the service or

product they are offering.

Most of us in business spend so much time learning and focusing on areas of our business that are not our skill sets, that we end up juggling many different hats.

I spent many years disillusioned and thinking that by achieving skills and qualifications I would be successful – setting me apart from my competitors and being an expert in my field.

How wrong was I?

Even though my narrow-minded approach was fundamental in estab-

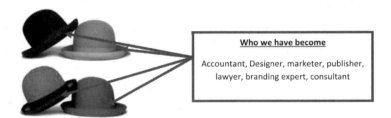

lishing my reputation as an expert and helping my clients improve their business' performance and profits, it occurred to me some years back now that I had not focused as much on my family balance skills along the way.

I found at an early stage of my business the biggest stumbling block to my family and business balance success was?

ME!!!

I look at myself and did an assessment:

✓ Am I genuinely interested in my family's and business needs? YES.

✓ Do I have fun and have regular contact with the family and business clients? YES.

✓ Do I have connection time with the husband and down time for me? YES.

✓ Am I a good listener? Do I encourage my children and husband to talk about themselves? Do I encourage my clients to talk about themselves? YES.

✓ Do I make my children and husband and my clients feel important – and do it sincerely? YES.

If you have not done ALL the above, all is not lost. You can turn things around using time-tested strategies. It's all within your control.

The key is to be authentic and engaging with people. Listen and truly care about your families and clients. They will warm to this and will be more likely to support your business 'way' into the future.

Take a look in the mirror. I did, and it made a huge difference to how I conduct family and business now.

4. MAKING MONEY VS. FAMILY

Coming into the business world with a limited belief that being rich would take away time from your family is not true.

Making enough money in my Start-up phase was easy, as I knew what was required to support the family. However, my growth phase was difficult as the business was expanding rapidly, and these limiting beliefs that I previously held were starting to potentially have a negative effect on my family and business life. However with careful planning this was eliminated.

For some business owners, winning new contracts, gaining new customers indicate business growth with cash in the bank for some extravagant treats; this should have a positive effect on the family as you will have a lot more energy, time and money to spend on them.

5. WHAT GOALS HAVE YOU SET FOR YOUR BUSINESS?

I realised from the start that Goal-setting would be crucial to the success of my business, and is particularly important for business owners who can become distracted without focus. Goals direct actions, give you something to aim for, and can serve as a yardstick for measuring your business' success.

The way you approach goal-setting will determine whether you are able to attain your goals. Most people agree that goals are important, but less than five percent of people write down goals or have action plans for attaining them. Fear is most often the culprit. People don't like to write goals down on paper (a crucial part of goal setting) because they are afraid to commit to them. If this is your problem, try to remember that a goal can be changed at any time after you write it down. Also, keep in mind that goal-setting becomes easier the more times you undertake it. When you have set goals and attained them, the power of goal setting will compel you to set more.

✓ Have short-term and long-term goals

✓ Make your goals specific and measurable with a deadline

✓ Don't set yourself up for failure

✓ Don't be lazy

✓ Be relevant

✓ Be patient and persistent

✓ Review your goals constantly

If your business focuses changes, don't be afraid to alter your goals. Flexibility is a crucial component of goal-setting.

6. FUNDING YOUR BUSINESS

We became very proficient in a very short time, 12 months to be exact, as we identified our client's needs by working the plan and setting our goals.

Funding the expansion of my business was simplified, as it was a part of our goals we set as a family. This has played a major role in our clients businesses, on how they were also able to self-fund their expansion with little or no cash.

(a). Personal funding

Many start-up businesses believe they need a lot of capital; however this is not strictly true. Today, with good planning, you can start with zero funding. Various resources like your: savings, credit cards, equity in property or other options may be at your disposal.

(b). Friends and family

Obtaining loans from Friends and family can provide a quick resolution and give them great pleasure to support your business growth. On the other hand they may want to have a say in your business and this could cause resentment and relationship strains for all parties concerned.

7. CASE STUDIES

Failure is "REAL!!!" The consequences can be catastrophic; business should not be looked at lightly. These are true stories with real people like you and I, however the names have been changed to protect identities.

Start-up phase Annie

Annie had a start-up business, but over three months she became withdrawn with a sense of hopelessness, which was brought on by single handedly trying to balance her business and family commitments. After consulting with her family, she realised that they needed to seek professional counselling as they were going through a nightmare under the sheer weight of the new business.

Annie contacted us four months through her counselling as she felt that this wasn't the right route for her and her family. We were able to identify their problems and devised a simple 12-month plan with clear goals and objectives. They all thought that this was straightforward and easy to follow.

Growth-phase Jasmine

Money was a big issue for Jasmine, most nights were spent nerve-racking over the prospect of not being able to pay the next month's overheads to keep the business running; this made her quite depressed and disillusioned. She was thinking that affirmations sucked!

When Jasmine contacted us, we spent the first two weeks talking to her about her personal needs; this intern gave her back her confidence to share her anxieties about the business growth and direction, we set a plan and introduced her to many of our contacts so that she could reduce her expenses without getting rid of staff and plan a way forward.

These two scenarios are more common than we care to admit. There are people who have lost a lot or on the brink of losing everything because business is not shaping up as they expected. They are just holding on hoping the tide turns in their favour soon. You may be happy to know, Annie and Jasmine situations have improved with better financial management, planning and good old motivation.

There are people out there just like this who are working 80-hour weeks on their businesses and unable to spend time with loved ones they are trying to provide for. They literally hate the businesses they are running, and can't see any way out.

For most businesses, things could turnaround with a different approach. Having new insight and perspective from an outsider could change the business dynamics.

For those businesses that still have a pulse (some fighting chance for survival), I will be taking you by the hand and showing you exactly how to breathe life back into your company. You will have developed a newfound belief in yourself.

8. WHAT IS SO GOOD ABOUT WORK AND LIFE BALANCE FOR WOMEN?

Over the years we have supported many businesswomen and their families to reach that successful balance between work and family life. They follow our program – which involves the family. The business plan, which combines a clear definition and intentions of all the family members, allows you to put in place the structure of the business.

For example:

- How to plan family holidays around the business

- Develop excellent time-management skills

- How to limit business hours

- Involve family when needed.

We found that we were able to improve on their communication skills, giving all the family members a platform to air their concerns, if there were any. This intern generated trust and support, and with this in place, the business was able to flourish.

The experience of owning your business is gratifying and rewarding. We also make our clients aware that even though there are many positive points to running your own business, there are also risks to consider – which will require careful planning. Paying careful attention to your family needs with all things to consider will definitely balance your family and work life.

9. TOP TEN TIPS

1. **Family values**-having strong values can balance your business and family life.

2. **Talk about Responsibilities and Expectations.** Have family meetings, so that no one person has all the responsibilities and

does not lead to resentment. Having a routine in the home meant everyone had a share of the work, which was balanced.

3. **Time-management.** Being able to delegate and managing your time gives you back a portion of time for family life. Saying "NO" is priceless and a skill, but with practice will become easier.

4. **Refresh your schedule.** Your business may change as new opportunities come along and allow you to have more time.

5. **Balancing-scale between family and work.** This is an ongoing process and does not happen automatically. Accepting this can reduce disappointment and facilitate you to have power over this practice.

6. **Procrastination.** Stress can be due to working unproductive hours and what could be done in 5 hours may take as long as 8 hours. Less procrastination equals more time for family.

7. **Keeping abreast of Family Goals.** The family goals will change overtime as the need becomes greater, and the opportunities to spend quality time together playing, doing projects with them won't be there forever. Make the decision to know what's important, and writing it down will give you the assurance that it will happen.

8. **Identify the Pay-off of Balance.** Identifying the balance will really set the scale, the home, children, husband and business. This will help you forge a lasting relationship with each.

9. **Identify Imbalance.** It is essential to be aware that your business priorities are your responsibilities and that they may sometimes have to come first before family.

10. **What can W.A.L.B. for women do for you?** Balancing work and family can be hard to grasp. We will set priorities with you, find the resources needed, help you gain skills and become more assertive in your decision making, and help you identify the family needs and aspirations. This will give you the confidence to say, "I have found the right balance and it works."

10. CONCLUSION

The one secret that I can leave you with is that you never stop reaching for the best for you and your families, as the rewards that you will gain are priceless.

There is no catch to our methods and it is quite a simple step-by-step formula, so that using it anyone will be able to achieve this.

About Sapphire

Sapphire Gray currently lives and works in London, England and graduated with three degrees from The University of East London and London Guildhall (now named Metropolitan University) despite being dyslexic. Sapphire is critically acclaimed as the "Work & Life Balance for women" Expert.

Sapphire's expertise is in demand from women business centres, start-up enterprises, businesses looking to increase their profits and business hubs at universities. Sapphire consults and gives advice to business women on how to balance family life with a busy working schedule. Sapphire has been interviewed numerous times by local and international businesses regarding her own experience of balancing a busy work schedule with family life. Sapphire's aim is to use her experience and knowledge to help women achieve the right balance in terms of work and personal relationships.

In 2004 Sapphire founded what has now become "Work & Life Balance for women" and taken it from a local business to international status. Her clients regard her as the leading expert in this field.

She provides the skills to set up and maintain a profitable business, and offers a membership site that takes her clients through a weekly program full of various resources, help sheets, coaching packages, business rolodex, and more... A major part of the program is accountability in the form of a monthly progress report that she provides for her clients. She has a powerful system that works and creates positive results.

Here are what a few of her clients had to say about her:

Angel Thomas: In2Equity Financial Services: *"Great at problem solving and finding solutions, I have found her to be honest, trustworthy."*

Flavia Gregoire: Mentor Scheme Officer at University of East London: *"Sapphire is a very strong individual with the heart for others – determined to make a difference in their lives."*

Valrie Stewart-Executive Mentor... *"Sapphire Gray is an ideal person with strong follow through, who can be relied upon to deliver to the stated requirements of the given individual, situation or event."*

Sapphire's clients are diverse in background, education, the type of businesses they run and the relationships they have - but all have benefited from her experience and personalized advice, which is designed to focus on each individuals unique needs.

NEW RULES OF SUCCESS

To learn more about Sapphire Gray's Work-Life-Balance for women and how you can receive a special report, "The top 10 powerful reasons why balancing your family & business make you more money."

Visit: www.worklifebalanceforwomen.com

Email: info@worklifebalanceforwomen.com

Office free phone: 0800-612-8816

CHAPTER 19

SUCCESS TO AND THROUGH RETIREMENT

BY RON CAMPBELL

Success, just like money, means different things to different people. To some, it may strictly be about the money. Family, personal, health – it doesn't matter – to me, that just doesn't cut it. I'm greedy, I want it all; fame, fortune, family and friends - I want it all. I'd like to tell you it's easy, but it's not. It is going to take a lot of work, but with the right direction and intent, you can get there. The late, great Zig Ziglar used to say, "You can get everything in life you want if you just help enough other people get what they want."

As a father of four daughters, I used to preach, "Education first, career second, fall in love third." If you get the order right, it is much easier for everything else to fall in place. I have been very fortunate as a financial advisor to meet and work with people from various walks of life. On both a professional and personal level, I've seen just about everything there is to see, yet, I'm still learning every day what it not only takes to succeed, but also about the pitfalls that can sabotage your desired results. That's probably the 1st lesson – and from which the learning doesn't stop just because you've graduated from school. It's been said that this is when the real learning begins.

An example of having it all can be found by observing Adrian and Catina B_____. This is a couple that I have a lot of admiration and respect for because of the way they conduct themselves in their everyday lives.

Catina happens to be my oldest daughter and Adrian is my son-in-law, so their story is close to my heart. They both got good educations first, and then started their journey towards building a successful career. My daughter has always been very goal-oriented so anyone that would be able to get close to her would exhibit those same personality traits. Adrian was and is a gentleman first and foremost, (which is something that made me happy), and that lies in good part to the success of his parents. The parents play a most important role but the descendants have to follow through. In the 10+ years since they married, they're well on their way to having it all! Adrian left his successful career and is now part owner of a software company. Catina has put her business career on hold to be a stay-at-home mom. This is where they really shine. Work is easy; raising kids is the tough part! In the case of the B____'s, dad has his busy work schedule that comes with frequent traveling, as well as the beautiful twin girls, Stella and Sophia, and their handsome little man Dimitri, that come with school, church, and sports activities to juggle.

Among the many hats they wear, Adrian and Catina are also a son and daughter, aunt and uncle, brother and sister, good friend, and so on. You get the point that there are tons of roles they fulfill – each one demanding time and attention – making distractions a constant part of their lives. It takes careful planning and execution to keep these things in check and enable continued progress towards one's goals. I've witnessed first-hand, the discipline of nurturing these three blessings and how those little angels take breaks from playing just to come and get a hug or kiss from Mom and Dad. That affection is proof that this couple understands the quality of time is more important than quantity. With a gorgeous home and a vacation home that the five of them visit when possible, Adrian and Catina are well on their way to having it all. Some will say I'm partial because they are family and that may be true, but it doesn't change the fact of what they have accomplished. There is much to be learned from this well-respected couple.

So, if we can agree that the learning never stops and it's going to take a lot of hard work and sacrifice, where do you begin? One of the things you need to determine is your path; are you going for a career? …And if so, what profession? …Or are you going the self-employment route? Perhaps that will be answered by your why. Why are you doing what you are doing? Did something from your childhood make a lasting impression? Was there an event, good or bad that influenced your direction?

Or is it something from within that is giving you a sense of purpose. My story began by seeing my Granny and her daughters and daughters-in-law get in a very good mood at the beginning of the month when the mailman would bring something called a social security check. Back then, kids were to be seen and not heard, so I only wondered to myself, "Why don't they get him to bring a social security check EVERY week of the month instead of ONE week a month? Then they would be happy all of the time."

As I got into high school, I realized what social security was and how Granny lived with us from time to time not because she WANTED to, but because she HAD to – it was our parent's turn to take care of her. Of course, with Granny came the social security check. I also thought it was horrible that people, after working hard their entire lives, basically retired to the poverty level and lived a very meager retirement. I don't think people took much notice because the average person made it ap- proximately three years in retirement before dying. In my case, my dad collected 11 social security and pension checks before passing away. But, as I am writing this, my mom is 96 years old and STILL collecting social security. So I have seen both sides of the coin.

When speaking of new rules, social security and pensions are probably not going to play the part in your financial success that it has in the past. The old rules were referred to as the 3-legged stool – social security, pension and personal savings. The new rules are going to be mainly personal savings and holdings, or better referred to as the *YO-YO* method – *You're On Your Own*. This alone is going to require a whole new approach. Keep reading. By the end of this chapter, I'm going to direct you to resources to not only help you survive in any economy, but to actually THRIVE. The good part is that by harnessing what people before you have done and are still doing, you don't have to reinvent the wheel.

I hope by the time you finish reading this chapter you will have more questions, because that will tell me you are beginning to think. I tell people at workshop events I lead that if you leave with more questions than when you got here, that they are beginning to think and that is a good thing.

The financial industry as a whole is good at telling people what to think instead of how to think, because they then lead them to products and services that serve the industry at the expense of those same people. Just witness the various changes, surcharges, fees, expenses, taxes, and penalties that you encounter in your everyday dealings. But I don't want to get ahead of myself. The financial information I share will put a nice bow around the success strategies to help you jumpstart your future.

I recall a discussion with a client quite a while ago and he asked how I got to the point I was at. You see he was venturing into a career change out of necessity. He was losing his job. So, as we looked at his options and that question came up, I shared with him how I was fortunate to find someone, a mentor, maybe a little older and I started learning from him. We discussed how that could speed up the process because as the saying goes, "The smart man learns from his mistakes, BUT the wise man learns from someone else's mistakes."

Another resource I advised my client to use was Michael Gerber's *E-Myth Revisited*. If you are going the self-employment or business owner route, this is a must read. In this great book, Mr. Gerber shared how AT&T coined the phrase "The System is the Solution." My client murmured "Wow" in a hushed tone, that prior to my encounter with Mr. Gerber's book, while I was busy meeting and advising clients, my secretary was filing, processing business and answering the phones among the various office duties according to her previous training and perceptions. This worked fine until she was out sick, quit, retired, or fired. Then the next administrator would come in and a whole new process would begin. It was kind of like two steps forward and one step back or spinning my wheels.

In writing our manual, we broke down each task from greeting clients to advertising and generating financial plans, and systematized each step in the process with a written process and checklist. Now, if someone was out of the office, the show could still go on. It also meant that any new hire would know what their exact duties would be and they could be held accountable. I said to my client Jerry, "My team knows we are working for a common goal and if it is not working, we will tweak or change the system. They will not be responsible for any lack of progress." However, with that said, if they are unable or unwilling to follow the system, they will be terminated. No exceptions. They know this up front and sign an agreement as such.

I told Jerry that "the fire hose" comes in seven steps:

1. Constant learning

2. Hard work

3. Figuring out your why

4. Finding a mentor, coach or someone to copy (learning from others)

5. Being alert to your perceptions

6. Staying motivated

7. Systems for everything

Another challenge we all face, no matter where on the path of success you reside, is that, in the U.S., we have an aging population, a declining workforce and a broken government. With 78 million Baby Boomers now in the entitlement line, (with me being one of them), the government will be pulling out all of the stops to honor their obligations. Translation: higher taxes at the very least. Make no doubt about it, we are going to pay. Think about it. If a politician gets elected by saying he's only going to raise taxes on the big corporations, and then he actually does what he says (hey, that may be a first), what are the big corporations going to do? Of course, raise the prices of their goods and services and pass those increases right along to us. It happens all of the time. When the sign on the back of a 'semi' reads, "This vehicle paid $8,120 in highway taxes last year," do you think the company paid it out of their end or do you think it was passed to us? You know the answer. Sometimes it's out in the open such as when fuel costs spike, and my airline ticket adds a surcharge passing the fuel increase along to us.

Let's look at one of the government's strategy for collecting more revenue. Imagine you are going to purchase something, let's just say a car. After doing your normal test-driving, various color combination, options and features checks, you find exactly what you're looking for. Now, the last deciding factor: price. What are you going to pay? In answering the question, suppose the dealer said, "You know we're sitting pretty well right now. You go ahead and enjoy your new car and in six months to a year from now, we'll send you a bill based on what we need at that time." You see, you could pay now, or take the chance of paying more or less in the future. You'd make your decision on what you thought the future might bring based on facts and information you have now. If you thought the company would continue their good fortune and prices may be lower, you would probably defer. If not, you'd pay now to avoid any surprises in the future.

Now compare that to a government sponsored IRA, 401(K), 403(B), or SEP IRA. These plans are sold as tax deductions in the current year, but they are really tax-deferred plans. You will eventually pay the tax. Based on the current fiscal condition of our country and the changing demographics, where do you think taxes reside in the future, higher or lower? The perception of these plans is that you will retire to a lower tax bracket. The reality is: most successful retirees are paying more income taxes than ever before. Also don't forget the penalties on their accounts. Now, I'm not saying don't put money in those plans, I'm saying consult with a qualified financial person who can compare the pros and cons with alternative plans that you might not know even exist.

Now your money has to reside somewhere and I'm going to share with you how to make sure all your success doesn't go to someone else, all because you didn't manage your money in the most efficient way available!

Nelson Nash, a colleague and friend of mine, discovered a life-changing financial strategy decades ago and shared it in his book, *Becoming your own Banker*. Mr. Nash states everyone needs to be in two businesses, their own profession and the banking business. This book needs to be added to your library and read and re-read several times to fully absorb and appreciate the potential. The web address is: www.infinitebanking. org where you can order the book and also view videos on this strategy. Nelson explains in this groundbreaking book that there is nothing greater in life than man's need for finance. It's what makes the world go around. He demonstrates by utilizing a financial vehicle that's been around for 200 years. You can eventually control the banking function in your life and reap the same benefits that banks have always enjoyed. It doesn't happen overnight but it will happen. When it does, you will have a pool of capital that continues it to grow, whether you're using it or not, and it has the potential to grow to a small fortune over your lifetime. It's simple, but not easy. In addition, this strategy removes the element of stock market risk and taxes both now and in the future. Of course tax laws are always changing so by the time you read this, or get around to doing something about it, the same potential may not exist. That's why you need to work with a financial professional well-versed in this area.

This strategy is currently allowing many of my clients' access to their money without taxes or penalties no matter their age and there are no loan applications to fill out. They have liquidity use and control (LUC) and now think in terms of lost opportunity cost (LOC) when considering any financial opportunity.

This strategy alone is sometimes responsible for bringing all your hard work together, allowing you to take advantage of opportunities over your lifetime that otherwise may pass you by. Don't miss out on this most incredible potentially lucrative strategy that may require you to 'think outside the box,' depending on any pre-conceived notions you may have.

Just think, contemplate and reflect. There may be more within your reach than you ever imagined.

About Ron

Ron Campbell, CFP®, RFC®, is the founder and principal of Campbell Financial Services. He has over 35 years of "in the trenches" experience in the financial services industry. He has served as an adjunct faculty member for adult education in financial planning at various high schools and community colleges, and has also taught those same courses at several companies. Ron has served as host of radio's *Successful Business Hour* and has been quoted and published in various publications. He also hosts "Talkin' Money with Ron" on the Retirement Radio Network.

Ron was featured as part of America's Premier Experts TV Show "The Consumers Advocate" which airs on ABC, NBC, CBS and Fox affiliates. He has also been seen in *Forbes, Newsweek* and *The Suit* magazines. By the Commonwealth of Kentucky, Ron has been commissioned a Kentucky Colonel.

In specializing with retirees or those about to be retired, Mr. Campbell utilizes strategies that focus on guaranteed income and preservation of capital. What worked in the accumulation phase of one's life may not work as well during the distribution phase. Mr. Campbell believes when it comes to investing, there is more to be gained by avoiding losses rather than picking the apparent winners. With the changing demographics and our country's fiscal woes, Ron believes risk, taxes, penalties and inflation need to be considered before implementing any investment strategy.

Memberships include The Better Business Bureau®, Financial Planning Association®, International Association of Registered Financial Consultants®, and Wealth and Wisdom®.

Ron and his wife Cheryl are the proud parents of four daughters and one son-in-law. Ron is the proud "Poppy" to seven beautiful grandchildren.

To schedule a time to discuss your financial future, contact them at:
Ron@RonCampbell.net

Or call (410) 766-0900 today!

Campbell Financial Services
7310 Ritchie Highway, Suite 700 Glen Burnie, MD 21061
Phone (410)766-0900   Fax (410)766-0908
www.RonCampbell.net

CHAPTER 20

GOT SUPERPOWERS?

BY VICTORIA COMFORT

"The mind is a terrible thing to waste" was once quoted during an iconic campaign used by the United Negro College Fund to drive home the point of the necessity of education. I'm sure most of us would agree with that statement. We can probably also agree that as humans, we are just tapping into the true power of our magnificent minds. Imagination is one aspect of the mind, as are Memory, Intention, Opinion and Feeling, but for now, let's focus on Imagination. The mind cannot create something out of nothing without the imagination, but have you really considered the powers of imagination in how we create our reality? Just take a moment to consider this. Throughout the history of mankind we have created new truths (the earth being round instead of flat for example), new tools, and new possibilities that had not yet been conceived through the powers of the imagination. We create something out of nothing by imagining. We create something not yet created with the imagination, we follow a course of action to make the imagined real and we achieve success. Or do we? Is success achieved through our actions or through our imagination? I would argue that success is achieved through the imagination and that we create our own reality, success or failure, by how we use our imagination. Our imagination is the superpower of our minds!

Just about every kid imagines being a superhero or having superpowers. My kids have often asked the question of each other, "If you could have one superpower, what would it be?" I must admit, I was surprised one evening when they asked me what superpower I would like to have. I really hadn't thought about superheroes or superpowers in all of my adult life, it's all just the imaginary world of a child after all. We grow up, get jobs and work on our careers, start families, and pay bills... Imagination takes a backseat to being a responsible, respectable adult. Why take valuable time to partake in frivolous dreams and imaginary nonsense, I've got work to do! They asked the question again, "Come on Mom, pick a superpower." I felt a little silly at first and I really wasn't aware of all the superpowers that I had to choose from. Would I want to be invisible, to fly, super strength, walk through walls... I can't even recount all the superpowers my kids came up with, but I reluctantly considered all my superpowers options and chose one so we could move on. Hopefully my answer, to be invisible, would satisfy them and I could go back to thinking about all that I had to get done the next day. The kids would not accept my short answer and asked me more questions. "Why invisible? Would you be invisible all the time? What would you do while invisible?" So many questions about some superpower that I was never going to have so why put so much thought and energy into it?

The question kept coming up from my kids, in the car, at the dinner table, in the doctor's office waiting room. It was a consistent topic of conversation for a while. I had become used to the question, expected it and in fact, I started to enjoy answering it. I was fun to think about and it was a brief escape from being a responsible adult. As I was starting to feel better about answering the question I noticed that I was posing the superpowers question to myself without my kids even asking. My imagination, if only for a few moments, gave me the freedom to feel different from the day-to-day struggles I was experiencing.

At the time, I was not a happy or successful individual in any area of my life. I was "burning in my own little hell" as I used to say. Ugly divorce, total loss of income, raising two children alone... I had so much on my plate that I didn't like or didn't want, but I couldn't seem to change any of it for the better. I thought I had done everything right in my life to achieve success. I worked hard at my career, worked at being the best wife, mother and daughter... I should have had it all but the end result was hardly a success, and in fact, I considered myself a complete failure! They say that misery loves company and I was sure to let everyone know how miserable I was, how hard things were for me.

I was so consumed by my misery and how I was going to survive that it became my entire life. The more I thought about how useless I was, the more useless I became. The more useless I became, the more I thought about how useless I was and the cycle would repeat itself, over and over, and over. I was super-powerless. The negative thoughts and images I had of myself and my life became all-consuming and everything seemed to continue to get worse. I kept thinking that things could not get any worse but yet, they did. I was confused, defeated and terribly unhappy all the time. Superpowers? Nonsense!

I was irritable and bothered by having to answer such a silly question the first time but each time I answered it I began to notice something changing in me. I was starting to feel different, not so miserable. I looked forward to escaping from my misery for those few minutes with my kids, those minutes of escape into my imagination. I continued to imagine and dream up all sorts of wild and wonderful scenarios with my new-found superpowers and I started to feel even better. As I began to feel better, things started to get better. The better I felt, the better things became. The more I allowed my mind to experience the feelings of being super powerful, the more powerful I became. The grief and challenges I was facing started to become manageable and life wasn't looking as grim as it had before. I was even seeing some success in my life where before all I could see was failure.

Who would have thought that a question from children about having superpowers would be the catalyst for my attaining joy, success and true fulfillment? How did this one question move me from despair to hope? What did I learn from the mind of a child that changed everything? When did the change happen and is this something anyone can do? Yes and again, it is so simple, anyone can do it plus it's a lot of fun. Let's start with the mind of a child.

When we are young, it is expected that we will dream and imagine fantastic, unbelievable things. Much of our young life we are living through our imagination, free to desire being a policeman, a teacher, a doctor, or Superman! Just asking a child the question, "What would you like to be when you grow up?" can illicit a fifteen minute monologue from the child…about how they want to be a fireman who goes into buildings that have huge flames and smoke, but the fireman is ok because he has a mask and a big fire hose that shoots out water on the fire… It's quite entertaining to listen to their dreams. Their imaginations are limitless! There are no boundaries of possibility, no thoughts of whether or not what they imagine is even possible for them to achieve. They are free to allow their imagination to take them anywhere, anytime. They are free to believe their imaginations can become real and they can actually feel with their emotions that they are living the image. Then we grow up.

As we grow, imagination takes a back seat to reality. We live according to what is, what we can see, what we can prove and what we expect. We aren't encouraged to look too far beyond that. We have boundaries placed on our imagination as adults that didn't exist when we were children. As adults, we still use our imagination but certainly not with the freedom we had as children, and we often don't dare to imagine beyond the scope of reality. This lack of freedom, these boundaries, enslave our mind, define our possibilities and confine us to limited beliefs about ourselves and life in general. We have exchanged our limitless imagination for a limited reality and only believe what's possible through those realities. As a result, most of us are creating only what seems realistic to our thinking mind – instead of creating what is possible from our imagination mind. So what is different about creating from an unlimited imagination and how can we use it to propel us toward our greatest achievements?

When we imagine something it triggers certain feelings. It doesn't matter what we imagine, we will feel something as a result. If we imagine something we view as negative, we feel bad. When we imagine something we view as positive, we feel good. Certain neurons are fired communicating to the brain the image and the feeling and the body responds as a result. Imagine there is a knock on your door right now and a man is standing there with a check for you for a million dollars, no strings attached. What is the first feeling you have in that moment? Most of us would feel elated! How would your body respond to the elation? Your heartbeat might quicken, you may smile or you might start jumping up and down unconsciously. Your imagination created a feeling in your body. What did you feel? Now suppose there is a knock on your door right now and a man is standing there with a debt he needs to collect from you, but you don't have the money to pay it. How do you feel in that moment? Most of us would feel nervous, agitated or scared, and our bodies would respond by breaking out in a sweat or we might have a sinking feeling in our stomach. Feel the differences in yourself in these two instances, just by what you are imagining. Notice your body responding in certain ways to these images. How does it respond in each instance? Do you have to think or tell your heart to beat faster? No, it just responds to the images currently in your mind and the feelings created from those images.

Whether you engage the neural pathways in the brain through imagination or action, the same motor and sensory programs in the brain are used. Positive mental practice (imagination, visualization) has been used as an effective method to prepare for a physical skill. These days most professional athletes use some form of mental practice in addition to physical practice, because it helps them to achieve better performance. Each thought changes the structure and function of the brain by affecting the neurons at a microscopic level. A runner for example, might visualize crossing the finish line of his event three seconds faster than he has ever done before. He is training his brain to respond to the visualization so that when the action occurs, the neurons responsible for movement instruction are influencing his physical result. In essence, the mind has already practiced through the imagination, so the body is better able to respond to the instructions. The imagination of performing better than before influences the body to perform better than it has before. What we imagine strengthens the neural pathways for success or failure, and it influences our results.

When you imagine having superpowers or being super-powerful, your mind registers your feelings and creates a pathway for achieving success. The beauty of this technique is that it works for virtually any challenge you need to overcome. Are you nervous about an interview with a potential employer? Imagine going into the interview with superpowers. What superpowers would you have? How would they help you perform your best in the interview? How do you feel when you imagine having these superpowers? Now put yourself having these powers in front of the person interviewing you. Imagine yourself being so super powerful that there is no question you can't answer, and your power and ability are clearly superior. Feel how powerful, unstoppable, and capable you are. Still feeling nervous? Now let's break this down into five easy and fun steps anyone can do to train their brain for success:

1. Find a quiet place where you won't be disturbed and get comfortable. This exercise can be as short or as long as you have time for.

NEW RULES OF SUCCESS

2. Bring to your mind any challenge, idea, conflict or goal for which you have the desired outcome you wish to achieve, or better. Be specific! The more clear you are about the desired outcome or one that is even better, the more specifically you will train your brain toward the desired outcome or better.

3. Imagine you have every power necessary, superpowers even, to accomplish the desired outcome or better. Imagine how powerful, brilliant, focused and capable you are of achieving your desired outcome, or better. Imagine with gusto and imagine without boundaries.

4. Become aware of your feelings as you are imagining. Allow only positive feelings to enter your body as you imagine. Feel how happy, strong, confident and unlimited you are! Feel deeply! How great can you make yourself feel through the power of your imagination?

5. Close the exercise with gratitude and give thanks to the beautiful, unlimited, powerful imagination you have.

Did you have fun on your imagination road trip? Are you feeling better than you did prior to doing the exercise? Keep practicing and strengthening your imagination muscle and you will experience more success than you had before. I still imagine what it would be like to be invisible from time to time although my kids stopped asking me about superpowers some time ago – but if they were to ask, I would tell them that I already have a superpower, the superpower of the mind, my imagination.

About Victoria

Victoria Comfort has nourished thousands of people as a Chef, Recipe Developer and Food Stylist. She has been cooking for over 25 years for celebrities, athletes, politicians, executives and families – as well as developing and styling recipes for national brands, magazines, cookbooks and Networks.

Using her in-depth knowledge and understanding of relationships in and out of the workplace throughout her career, education and life experience, she began her coaching and healing practice. She has founded gps-2-success.com and is a best-selling author and speaker.

She is currently writing *Soul Compass True North*, living your truth using the compass within, and, *Soul Compass Magnetic North*, aligning your compass to the best possible outcome. She lives in Northern California with her two children.

CHAPTER 21

MINDSET COMES BEFORE SUCCESS

BY GREGORY PIERRE-LOUIS

When we mention "success" the first thoughts might seem a bit intimidating or daunting, but really ask yourself, "What is success?" Many things in life, for example our actions and the decisions we make, are all based on and lead back to an origin – the root. Being able to wrap your mind around this perspective and concept will allow you to explore a whole new realm of personal growth. It allows you to make sense of the ends justifying the means, and to make adjustments to be better and do better, overall improving and expanding on your personal development. It creates a quantifiable and traceable way to locate weaknesses in areas that are holding you back from achieving your dreams. You want to be assured that you know how to control and manage the machine or tool that is going to help you to make all of your goals attainable, reaching the level(s) of success that you've only ever really dreamed of – up to this point in your life.

Mindset is an important aspect of success, and so is confidence; moreover, believing in yourself and what you do is everything. Most people get stuck "in their ways," and tend to settle for what seems to be the "norm." The world is ours to make what we want of it – but that requires work, planning, commitment, growth, and most importantly, the right state of mind. When I began to really master my thoughts, actions, and directing my future successes, I turned to the Internet to spread my positive influences in a viral manner. It was my gateway to masses of people from all walks of life on this beautiful and unique earth. Seeing results from the hard work, passion, planning and action that you take and make, is probably one of the most amazing emotions you can ever experience in your life. Once you get a taste of your work paying off, and observe the traction starts to build, do not hesitate or get frightened by the idea of not knowing what is about to happen. Instead, just allow the momentum of what you're doing correctly to drive you and your goals to the next steps of success. People are often afraid of stepping out of their comfort zone, but being successful is out of everyone's comfort zone in the beginning. Nobody is just born successful. It's something that they once did not have, yet achieved. Something that they had to get used to, but more importantly, it is also something that they were not afraid of. A good idea to implement to get better at expanding the boundaries of your comfort zone is to be open to new concepts, ideas, and perspectives. It will be the driving force behind expanding your goals overall.

To know that struggle is naturally a part of life is important, and should never be a hidden thought or factor when mentioning the idea of becoming successful. This should always be in the forefront of your mind. The more you understand and accept this reality, the easier it is to deal with the bumps in the road when they do happen, because they WILL happen at some time or another. The ability to maintain and remain being mentally, emotionally, and physically strong is a characteristic of leadership and success, one that those who are fortunate enough to reach that particular level of being successful to say that they "made it" tend to leave out. I refuse to do you any such injustice. The more those "successful" individuals spread the knowledge and truths about what it really takes to reach your goals, without creating and fabricating fluff, and revealing the raw real-life experiences and naked facts about the many different paths to success, the more that we, as a people, can avoid or at least try to avoid making the same mistakes and going through the same hardships as those who have truly successfully done it prior. They say the best way to learn is to model after those who have done it before you, but the important key to remember is exactly how they did it. Observe, take notes, absorb the knowledge and implement it into your life and your path towards success and your dreams.

When I look back, there were many times throughout the day I used to ask myself, "What can I do better?" That exact question is what changed my life because I know what the answer is now. Better yet, I put it to practice

EVERY SINGLE DAY! There comes a time in your life when you have to make a decision on what it is you really want. If you truly understand this, you can begin to tap into the realm of self-empowerment, allowing you to develop and mold the correct mindset and ultimately grooming the best habits for achieving success. Personally, helping people is not just one of my passions, it makes life worth living, and is also secretly exhilarating.

Working as a Paramedic in New York is the way I used to put this passion into practice. It allowed me to realize that I truly enjoy making a difference in other people's lives until it became clear to me that there was a problem in my approach. The issue was my inability to reach a larger number of people to influence and help. I was limited to being one person, working on one ambulance, helping one life at a time. Until one day, sending an email to my organization, a light bulb went off in my head. Quickly, everything made sense, as the answer stared me dead in the face...THE INTERNET! The World Wide Web was my answer to touching the lives of more people on a much larger scale.

At that very moment, I knew that starting Webit Marketing Inc., also known as Team Webit, was my next big venture in life. It was like divine intervention. Whether you know it or not, every second that passes we mentally re-analyze, re-assess, and re-configure our actions and goals based on our environment or any changes that occur. A little bit of inspiration, guidance and support can take anyone a long way in acheiving their goals and ultimately being successful. This reason alone is why I decided to model the company around the entire concept of *teaching, helping, inspiring*, and *supporting* individuals, businesses, and organizations.

Zig Ziglar once said, "You will get all you want in life, if you help enough other people get what they want." This is something that I strongly believe. Webit Marketing Inc models this concept by helping business owners, firstly, by showing where they stand with their business, secondly, by educating them on what it is that they need to do to improve the areas of their business that fall short, and lastly, providing the tools and resources for them to grow their businesses exponentially when it comes to marketing. As a result, the individuals themselves live a life of freedom and passion. Ultimately, this provides a better quality of life for anyone within that network.

Local people in the community work for these businesses to provide for their families, and are involved with the schools, charities, non-profits, sports leagues, Chambers of Commerce and other various clubs and organizations. The better off the businesses, institutions and organizations are, the better the lives of their employees and everyone involved, creating a happier network and a happier community. Understanding the Internet and the power behind utilizing it to help other people's lives has really helped me to fulfill my dreams of helping as many people as I can the way I know how. I know in my heart, that beyond just an idea, the passion that drives Team Webit influences the world in a positive way, and continually allows businesses as well as individuals to grow wholly. To possess such a power is truly a blessing. Moreover, to direct that power in the direction to help everyone else is a way of giving right back to a world that truly needs it.

I have never looked back since making the decision to live the life I've always wanted and dreamed of, which is doing what I love everyday and ultimately making a difference in the world. You must first understand how to think in a positive way, and learn how to implement that positivity in your life for these types of successes to occur. It goes without saying that this will require work and effort on each individual's part, however, it's well worth the sacrifice. It is up to you as a person to decide exactly how much effort you're willing to invest into yourself and/or your business. By grasping an idea of what you truly want, you can change your life and current situation, and pave your road to success – allowing those around you to begin to benefit from your positive aura as well.

Remember, the decisions you make directly reflect the paths you take in life. If you look at your brain as a road map, you can drive your future in any 'which' direction you want. That alone is probably one of the most powerful tools you can equip yourself with, as you mosey on through this journey they call life. As your mindset becomes more positive, your surroundings will appear to change. The power of positivity is tremendous and far from subtle. Things you did not notice before, you will find an appreciation for. People around you will feel it too. During these moments is when you'll realize *that your mindset is the key that drives the machine to success.*

Everything you think and do should begin to reflect all the positive energy flowing in and around you. If you find your thoughts drifting towards the negative, make every effort to turn back to positive. This might take time and practice, maybe even some help, but in the end, life through your eyes will seem so much clearer. Start paying attention to the way you carry yourself and the body language you use. Many people are conscious of other people's body language, and when your body language does not match the things you say, subconsciously, people lean towards the body language as being a more accurate reflective factor of your personality and character. Based on this little concept, people are misrepresented every day in their individuality, and moreover their social tier. So keep this in mind when setting impressions, or just how you carry yourself day-in and day-out.

"You get out what you put in." This is a quote heard time and time again, and seems to hold some truth with the concept of allowing your mindset to guide your life. If what you put in was positive, then it is likely that what you'll get out, for the most part, will be positive. Now that you see the potential of self-empowerment and creating your right mindset, you can see it's an idea worth putting into action. You have to be committed to the process, and allow yourself to grow into this new mindset. Once you get there, own it!

About Gregory

Gregory Pierre-Louis was born on August 14th in New York City, His parents, Marie Pierre and Wilson Pierre-Louis were natives of the Caribbean island formerly known as Hispaniola, particularly from the capital of Haiti known as Port-Au-Prince. He was raised an only child, and was not your typical rebellious teenager. As a teenage boy, he found solace in actively trying to understand the world around him, and adamantly attempted to get those closest to him to see the world through his eyes, influencing anyone around him by instilling positivity into them. At twenty-five, he had a spiritual awakening and began to pursue his writing and goals of entrepreneurship.

He determined early on that he wanted to be a writer and entrepreneur, but was discouraged by family, who saw no future in pursuing those goals. Gregory's non-rebellious adolescence allowed him to develop a great relationship with his parents. "As an adult, I can look back and not hold anything against my parents. They did what they thought was best for me, although most of the time, their strict cultural ways clashed with the modernized lifestyle of the Western Civilization that we live in. I grew up in a family that didn't just want you to be intelligent, but also intellectually curious. I was taught to have empathy for others and learned to empower my Self, ultimately leading to a healthy self-esteem."

After working in several professions, mostly healthcare related, Gregory changed his life's course and decided to become an entrepreneur. Now, Founder and President of three businesses based in New York, he feels that his outreach and goals of influencing the world positively are no longer limited. He even resigned from his other jobs, and devoted himself mostly to his businesses and the craft of writing. Many people find Gregory's writing to have a motivational and inspiring touch. He distinguishes himself by having a sense of what he calls "Self", making it a point for people to understand that when goals are set, they are to be pursued by what is in their heart for no one other than themselves, and not for the appeasement or happiness of anyone else. In an interview, Gregory states: "If people focused more on empowering themselves, they would have more substance to contribute to the world and making it a better place overall."

Since the launch of his businesses, Gregory Pierre-Louis' career has expanded exponentially. As a self-taught entrepreneur, Gregory was able to put together what seemed to be one-man business operations while working two full-time jobs. The success of these ventures have influenced his family, friends, acquaintances and many others to reach out to him. He has grown into a role-model and mentor, helping others with their personal issues, as well as any business advice he can offer. He aspires to start a charity one day to introduce modern technology to under-developed countries. Today, Gregory Pierre-Louis travels globally – sharing his story and teaching what he knows to other developing entrepreneurs and those interested in entrepreneurship.

Living what he calls "a blessed life", he is at home in New York, where he was born and raised, and he remains close to the loving family and friends who supported him in his journey and his ascent to entrepreneurial success.

CHAPTER 22

IS YOUR GLASS HALF FULL?

BY ROBERT CALTABIANO

How you look at life determines your destiny. Auto magnate, Henry Ford, said, "Whether you think you can, or you think you can't – you're right." When we visualize an image, our collective thoughts set in motion a process of emotion. The more clearly we envision something, the more emotion attaches to it; those emotions create an excitement that becomes a call to action to move toward the thing we strongly desire. By taking action, we become that about which we think. Wishing will not cut it. If you want to achieve something, you must believe in it yourself.

The age-old question "Is the glass half full or half empty?" takes on new meaning in the context of image. If the glass you see is half-empty, then the image you are allowing to take shape in your mind is only half of what you might achieve, in effect, lowering the bar for yourself.

It is only upon belief that you can do something or cannot do something that will bring about reality. Think about the saying "Be careful what you wish for." The process of calling into reality what you want by using your imagination does not know whether what you are wishing for is a positive or a negative. What you truly think and believe, can, in no uncertain terms, come true.

Radio personality Earl Nightingale spent most of his life studying and focusing on one thing…Attitude. In his famous work, "Lead the Field," Nightingale devoted his first lesson to that "magic word," Attitude. We are truly the sum total of our thoughts. Therefore, what you are thinking at this point reflects on the results you have been getting all your life. To quote Earl Nightingale "Great Attitude = great results, A good attitude = good results, Fair attitude = fair results and a Poor Attitude = poor results." "We become what we think about."

Since we are the sum total of our thoughts, to be truly successful we must take action upon what we truly want and reflect that towards our attitude. Our cup should always be half-full. Again, when we find ourselves down the path of poor attitude, we must seek to change our image of whom or what we are viewing, thereby calling on the positive results we are truly seeking.

Is there a process to success to encourage glass half-full imagery? Is there a magic formula that will transform your life, your business or your relationships? Yes, there is. There is an old adage that states, things are created twice, once in your mind and once in reality. Anything ever constructed by man was first a thought.

If you are entering a boardroom, you must envision yourself giving a successful presentation or talk. They may not buy what you are selling because of your technique or because of some other reason, but the fact is that what they will see is the positive belief in yourself. Every salesperson must first sell themselves, they must first see the sale in their conscious mind. We must not see with our eyes but with the inner eyes of understanding and imagination. Planted in the subconscious mind, the image can and only will take hold when coupled with the will to believe it. As adults, we struggle most of the time to replace our image, a negative thought for a positive thought. When we see ourselves and see our picture, we look from the outside in and not from the inside out. We develop fear.

DO NOT WORRY; FEAR IS THE NEGATIVE IN ACTION.

How do we change our worry or fear? Well, if we were to look at a newly-born child, they have no fear, no worry and really no anxiety. If they eat and have a clean bottom, they are happy campers. Yet over time, fear, doubt and worry creep in; planted into the conscious mind and then with an emotion transfer to the sub-conscious mind. In this way, we become what we think. A child, however, is open to all things positive and negative.

Think back to a time when you were in school and the teacher wrote on the chalkboard. When I imagine this, I can see myself, and the teacher, at a moment where my mind had wandered off to daydreams of wanting to be Babe Ruth and play baseball in the major league. The teacher would turn around--and see that I was not looking at the blackboard--and say, "Robert, pay attention." What she had just unconsciously done is drag me away from my imagination. Einstein said that, "imagination is more powerful than knowledge because knowledge is limited, but your imagination extends the universe."

Parents often say, "stop running!" or "Get off the couch, you are going to get hurt!" They unintentionally replace the child's image of his invincible self with an image of a fragile self and of fear. Parents don't do this consciously; they simply want to protect their children. Then the child's positive image rescinds into the image of adulthood, where fear, anxiety and confusion take hold and suddenly your cup is only half-full.

Most children readily exhibit positive attitudes. Anyone who has ever seen a child get giddy over ONE balloon has seen a positive attitude and a glass half-full mentality at work. An adult might see the balloon as "just" one balloon, but to a child with a positive mental attitude that balloon is a great treasure.

A child's thoughts span the realm of the universe; his mind is open to anything. That is why you can take a child of three years and younger and teach them languages so easily. They have a subconscious mind and imagination, and they become that about which they think. They become Barbie or a ballerina or Superman because they have no fear, and they do not have the conscious mind to tell them that they cannot be that. The image of the cup half-full does not exist for a child – the cup is FULL. You come into this world with a purity of thought that says I can do anything and be anything I want. As time goes by, based on our environment, based on our parents, based on husbands, wives, boyfriends and girlfriends, co-workers, the image starts to change and we put a hold on our imagination.

PLANT POSITIVE IMAGERY – DEVELOPING A HABIT OF INCREASE

None of us is born with fears or negative imagery. Parents often instill fear in their children in an effort to keep them safe from a world that the parent, not the child, perceives as big and scary. To overcome years of reprogramming toward fear, it is most advantageous to first disconnect from the negative voices around us and in our own heads.

Stop listening to the news: Negative sells in the news. A doom and gloom picture of the economy will not frame your workday in a positive light. Instead, consider that many businesses flourish in a down economy; replicate those.

Adopt an attitude of gratitude: Communicate with yourself and with others about all the things for which you are grateful. Picturing the wonderful things in your life can:

Change your Thinking: Have you noticed how few diets actually work? Depriving oneself of certain foods creates a negative environment. Weight loss success happens most frequently when a person changes the way he or she thinks about the process. Instead of looking in the cake and thinking, "I cannot eat that because I am overweight," choose instead to say "I am a healthy, strong person and if I choose to eat a little bit of cake it will not make me obese," or "I am choosing to eat healthier, therefore, I am not interested in eating that cake." You have to see yourself as you want to be seen by others. Either way, planting a positive image of health and strength will beat the negative image of being overweight and weak. Negative images are the rocks that weigh us down, and the seeds of success cannot take root and thrive in the rocks.

UNCONSCIOUS CONFIDENCE

Unconscious confidence can also be called the Midas touch. Everything that King Midas touched turned to gold. Certainly each of us has met at least one of those people about whom we shake our heads and marvel, "How can they be so lucky?" While it does not happen often, it is easy to recognize. Unconscious confidence occurs when something becomes so ingrained in a person that one no longer has to think about something. Did you have to think about how to get home from work or from the grocery today? Likely, you did not. The habit of driving home a particular way becomes so ingrained that sometimes you have no idea how you even got home. It's like autopilot. The key to success is making your success habit so ingrained that you do not have to consider what will be your next step on the ladder of success. The crux of unconscious confidence is concentrating so strongly on your ideal that pursuing it becomes a habit. Most people have to learn to concentrate.

CONCENTRATION TECHNIQUES

Concentration helps us to think. What we think about and envision will manifest itself in our lives. Therefore, it behooves us to learn to concentrate, really focus, on one task or element at a time. In this era of multi-tasking, computers, social media, wearing too many hats at work, many people are simply doing too many things at once. This is where the law of diminishing returns kicks in. At some point, everything suffers. Focus on one thing, your ideal, which is comprised of your goals and your priorities. You cannot "manage" time, but you can manage your goals and priorities one at a time.

During the Great Depression, an efficiency expert told the CEO of a company that he would give the CEO some advice on how to operate his company more effectively. After the CEO had determined what the advice was worth, only then would the efficiency expert be paid. The CEO figured he had nothing to lose, so he agreed and asked for the man's advice. The efficiency expert instructed the CEO to write down the top five priorities of what he has to accomplish each day. Prioritize means that item #1 should be the most important item of the day. He then instructed the CEO to do #1 on the list before anything else. Only when #1 had been completed was the CEO to begin item #2 on his list and so forth until his list had been completed. Furthermore, the CEO was challenged to give each item on the list his full attention while he was completing that item without trying to think about or act on the other items on the list.

Impossible right? In our multi-tasking society where we are "connected" everywhere 24/7, the idea of scratching items off a list seems as implausible as an ice rink in the desert, but it worked for that CEO. At the end of his experiment, the CEO's company had seen growth during one of the bleakest economic periods in history and the efficiency expert received a check for $25,000.

Remember what the efficiency expert said:

* *Prioritize*

• *Do ONE item at a time*

• *Cross the item off your list when completed*

We humans, well perhaps other animals do this too, tend to choose the path of least resistance. Our tendency is to quickly breeze through those tasks on our "to do" lists that can be accomplished quickly or while multitasking–dealing only with the minutiae of life and not those challenging matters that will offer a greater return on investment. While this approach might give the impression of having accomplished a great deal, it will invariably lead to more important tasks left unattempted, much less completed.

USING POSITIVE IMAGING FOR OTHERS

A person with a positive self-image should also have a positive image of others. A positive self-image will allow you to leave everyone with whom you come into contact to feel a sense of increase. Generally, you rise to the head of the company when you put good things out there that increase the abundance of others.

The Law of Polarity applies to the universe. Everything in the universe has an opposite: in and out, up and down, good and bad, left and right, right and wrong, and positive and negative. When confronted with a negative, realize that there must be a positive associated with it and seek the positive. Disasters and setbacks will happen. The difference between success and failure depends completely upon the imagining of a glass half-full and not half-empty.

A quick look at some American Presidents' use of imagery will illustrate the point. Let's begin with Franklin Delano Roosevelt. His fireside chats drew Americans to his side without his ever having to leave the comfort of the White House. FDR is purported to have actually envisioned himself speaking to each person individually as he made those addresses, and they responded in kind by seeing the picture as he created it. Alternatively, consider what President Ronald Reagan's "Shining City on a Hill"—his often-used image of America as he saw her place in the world—created for America. It offered Americans plagued by economic hardship and fears an image of an America that was not only untarnished but also a light to be raised higher for all to see. Wouldn't you like to elevate your business or your life to such a level? Finally, consider President Bill Clinton whose innate ability to leave people with a sense of increase for having been in his presence saw him through impeachment and scandals.

Whether selling a product or your abilities, you want to leave the room with the occupants feeling a sense of increase. Each of these presidents made a connection with the people whose lives they touched. Each of those presidents had a goal.

Despite our culture of instant gratification, real success comes with time, hard work and making positive connections with others:

- *Treat everyone as if he is the most important person in the world, because to them they are, and it is also the right thing to do.*

- *Shake a person's hand and mean it.*

- *Plant positives.*

- *Remember that you don't make the same connections with others by sitting behind a computer.*

GOAL SETTING, NOT GOAL CEILINGS

Growing up and working in New York City, I watched people fixated on their destination and trying to pile into taxicabs or city buses or on the subway trying to get somewhere. Most people never realized their true destination; they never reached it. A true destination is the road within us that has yet to be traveled because we are not aware of the road. Our road, a process of our beliefs and our thoughts, is placed on hold by external factors.

Earl Nightingale said, "Success is the progressive realization of a worthy goal" (or a worthy ideal). I like the word ideal better because an ideal is different from a goal. A goal is something you are planning that you want to achieve. An ideal is greater than that. An ideal is your whole makeup, your whole premise. What is your ideal, your premise? Ask yourself, "What do I want to be?" If you want to be successful, you must think of being successful and act it out in your mind, which will then resonate through your body. Pursue your ideal. Any goal that you set, that you think you can do, is not really a goal. A goal should be something that is so far out there, that it makes you so nervous that you are compelled to take action upon it. No one ever thought that Thomas Edison would succeed in creating the incandescent light. After 10,000 tries, he did it.

"Whether you think you can or can't, you're right." Only you can create the image you see in your mind. Only you can take the steps to take your image and make it reality. Absolutely everything without which we think we could not function today – cellphones, computers, coffee makers and flushable toilets – was created in someone's mind before it was manufactured in a factory.

Imagine your success, believe in it and set your new reality into motion and your glass to overflowing. When with constant space repetition of thought you can change your habits of old, change your old image and replace it with the one that you truly want. We do for sure become what we think about. What do you think about ?

About Robert

Robert Caltabiano is a Certified Life Success and Business Consultant/coach. Robert holds a B.S. in Criminal Justice/ Constitutional Law and is a 23-year veteran of the United States Secret Service who has received numerous letters of commendation from various Heads of State. His desire to assist and to serve others likely stems, at least in part, from growing up in the hotel and hospitality business.

Robert, a devotee of Earl Nightingale, coaches both business and personal clients toward becoming what they think about – helping them to "be" what they desire in their minds thus harnessing the power of imagery. Robert shares his insights into leadership and personal inspiration gleaned from years of working with, and learning from, several United States Presidents and from his very personal journey when his teenage son was battling and beating leukemia. Utilizing his years of experience in senior management and government leadership, Robert guides his clients through the process to success by encouraging them to discover and activate their hidden potential.

Robert is an enthusiastic public speaker and member of the National Speakers Association whose notable and diverse audiences include The United Nations, The United States Treasury and Homeland Security Departments, Major League Baseball, Bear Stearns, Citigroup, New York State Assembly and State University of New York, at Albany.

Marrying his passion for public speaking with his knowedge of the intricacies of human thinking, Robert became a certified "Thinking into Results" Consultant who assists individuals, organizations and businesses in uncovering their hidden strengths to achieve their full potential. Robert's own mentor and coach is Bob Proctor, whose ideas and theories are illustrated in the 2006 film "The Secret."

Robert is currently working on his first book related to successful living. When he is not coaching, speaking or writing, Robert fishes with his four children, listens to 1950's music and enjoys basketball and baseball. He is even a member of the North Texas Men's Baseball League. Robert is also a Certified Ocean Water Rescue Diver and instructor.

CHAPTER 23

THE NEW RULES OF SALES SUCCESS

BY PRESTON RAHN

Brendon was a twenty-five-year-old professional sales consultant who was determined to help grow his employer's company. Dr. Matt was a Chiropractor who wanted a better way to generate more business and revenue for his local practice. Tim was an Internet marketing consultant who wanted a better way to convert more prospects into his high-level private coaching program. These three people didn't know each other. They lived in separate parts of the country, they all had completely different types of clients and they all had completely different business models. Several things they had in common were the desire to make more money, to sell more of their products and services and to see more success in their businesses and their lives.

Millions of professionals struggle with the same problems that Brendon, Dr. Matt and Tim faced and feel stuck or frustrated in their own business and in their life. They try things that fail to bring them the level of success they envisioned in business and in their life. After trying many failed ways to convert more leads into a higher number of paying clients, they begin to doubt themselves and some even wonder if they're in the right business. Nothing could be further from the truth because success is not a secret. Success is a system. If you don't feel successful or see the level of success you envision in your life, then you are simply following the wrong system. Following outdated, ineffective and poor advice now will simply get you poor results in the future.

Do you want to make more money, sell more of your products or services, charge more than your competition and help as many people as possible succeed in their business and life? Are you a professional that gives an initial consultation to your potential prospects? Then, these "New Rules of Sales Success" are exactly what you want to study and master – because they will absolutely transform your business, your life and those of you who are in business to serve in a positive way. These steps have changed my life, they've changed many other people's lives, like Brendon, Dr. Matt and Tim, and they'll change your life too. In fact, with these New Rules of Sales Success you'll be able to help more people see and experience more success in their business and life while doubling or even tripling your sales and profits. Are you ready?

7 STEPS TO MASSIVE OFFLINE PROFITS

I'm no different than Brendon, Dr Matt or Tim and I'm no different than you. I struggled with sales and wondered what was wrong with me. I read books, attended seminars and even hired coaches. I felt that most methods were old, outdated and ineffective and most just didn't work. However, I did find some methods that did work and finally developed my own successful sales process. So, I didn't really invent these strategies, I just mixed a few together, added my own unique twists and finally created my own "secret sauce" that I call the "7 Steps to Massive Offline Profits."

The "7 Steps to Massive Offline Profits" that follow were created to make sure you start with a solid foundation in which to create, build and grow your profits quickly and easily. Whether you are a one-person entrepreneur, or have a complex sales cycle, it doesn't matter because these foundational steps can make all the difference between feeling stuck and becoming extremely successful. You're about to get the steps and the system. It's up to you to have the guts to take action and apply what you learn.

STEP 1: PRE-SALES AND MINDSET

To succeed you must have a system and the guts to take massive action. As one of my mentor's and good friends, Ken McArthur says, you need three things to be successful in business:

1. A product or service to sell.

2. An audience to sell it to.

3. You need conversion.

I can help you with the steps, the system and the conversion. It's up to you to figure out what you want to sell, who you want to sell it to and for you to have the guts to take action. I can show you the path. It's up to you to choose which path you want to take.

Your success really depends on how you see yourself because success comes from within. It's an inside job. It's an emotional agreement you have with yourself. If you have the drive and motivation and aren't seeing success, then you are probably just following the wrong system. The good news is that once you become "aware," you can make the choice to follow something new.

Now, there will always be bumps, roadblocks, obstacles and problems along the way and you may have to test out and try many new strategies and systems before you find something that works for you. Some things may work and some may not. Some may have aspects that feel good and other areas that just don't fit with you. Then you can do what I've done. Just take out the parts that resonate well with you and create your own "secret sauce."

Once you figure out and become aware of the path, the steps and the system, you'll be able to position yourself in a way where people will resonate with you and become attracted to you. This will create a shift in how people perceive you and will help you to begin the process of being able to convert more leads and prospects into more paying clients.

So, remember that you are the key to your success. When you build your success on a strong foundation, everything else will start to shift quickly and easily.

STEP 2: TWO MINUTE AGREEMENT

Once you have your mindset and heart-set on what you want, you've created a shift in how you position yourself and leads and prospects are starting to find you, you need to continue to position yourself as the leader and as the prize.

When you position yourself in a way where your clients see you as the prize instead of seeing themselves as the prize, it's really like the difference between you cold-calling someone and someone calling you. Can you see how the position changes in those scenarios?

In this second step, we continue positioning and leading by simply having a conversation with the prospect's subconscious part of the brain. Only a small part of the entire conversation is conscious or logical. We do this by simply setting the foundation for your time together with a "Two Minute Agreement," and where we set the ground rules for the appointment or call. Just as any game has rules to follow, you are doing the same thing here so everyone knows what's going to happen in the future and no surprises pop up.

Here's the formula I've developed to help you with your two minute agreement:

1. Position yourself as the leader.

2. Set the time frame or how long your appointment will last.

3. Set the agenda for the call or the "rules of the game."

4. Set the next step(s).

5. Create a verbal agreement with your prospect, which allows them to have a mental agreement with himself/herself.

These five steps can be presented in just two minutes and will separate you from your competition right from the start. This is a very short step that positions you to move easily into the next step, finding their emotional pain. However, it's a very critical step if you want to remove any "sales pressure" your prospect may bring in to your appointment and be in a better position for them to accept your offer later on.

The important part is that you must practice this step so that it's memorized, and so you are ready to perform at the right time. What usually happens is that we tend to slip right back into our old ways as soon as the call or appointment gets under way and we completely forget what we've previously learned. In order to avoid those old habits, we must practice over and over until it becomes a new habit and something that occurs naturally.

STEP 3: FIND EMOTIONAL PAIN

Why do we focus on finding emotional pain? We focus on finding emotional pain because people are more likely to take action now to relieve pain, rather than to take action on receiving pleasure or gain.

One of the easiest ways to find pain is to simply ask your prospects about it. People love to talk about their own life. When we ask open-ended questions, it allows people to communicate and helps us understand where they are now and where they want to be in the future.

Some open-ended questions might be as simple as asking someone where they are from. You can ask them about what they've done in the past, about why they are seeking someone to help them with their problem now, and where they want to be in the future once that problem is solved.

The idea is to create movement and contrast from where they were, where they are now and where they want to be. The gap that is created is where their pain lives. They want to be someplace in the future but don't know how to get there. That's the reason why my clients hire me, and that's the reason why your clients hire you. We may or may not be able to help them. We just don't know until we probe and ask. Asking open-ended questions helps us uncover and find their pain.

STEP 4: UNDERSTANDING THEIR PAIN

It's said that people won't go forward and do business with you unless they know that you understand them. When we empathize and even provide sympathy, that shows that we understand them and positions us as a possible solution to help solve their pain.

Your profits and sales depend on understanding and solving your prospect's and client's pain. When you can tap into and find out what they really want and why they want it, you are continuing to position yourself as the solution to their problem.

This is where you repeat back what they have told you they want, why they want it, and if you see a fit, allows you to transition into showing how you can specifically help them solve their pain.

STEP 5: OFFERING YOUR SOLUTION - THE "CLOSE"

It's said that if you need to "CLOSE" or if you need closing techniques, then you opened poorly. We don't teach people how to close deals. We teach people how to open relationships. When you can connect emotionally with people you won't need to close them because they'll simply close themselves.

If you've set the perspective with your two-minute agreement, asked the right open-ended questions, found their top one to three pains, and you can show them that you understand their pain, then you can easily just transition to your offer and simply ask them if they want to see how you can help them solve their pain. The more you ask the more sales you'll get. If you want to GET, you have to ASK.

We transition to our offer by a simple if… then… statement. For example, if we could help you with A, B and C, then, would that be valuable to you? This is not an open-ended question and forces either a yes or some other answer. If, at this point, their answer is anything other than "YES," you have not found enough pain for them to take action now.

If their answer is yes, then we just move on to the next step and show our offer. This is where we can compete on value and not on price. When we present different options it allows them to choose which one is best for them. When you only present one option or package their only other choice is to say "NO" or "I want to think it over."

After you present your options or packages, you can simply make a suggestion or a recommendation as to why you feel that option is the best fit for them. Then you can ask them which option they feel is the best fit for them at this time. Once you do, zip your lip and don't say a word.

The formula for presenting your offer and asking for the sale is as follows:

1. Transition with an 'If… Then…' statement

2. Offer your options

3. Recommendation and reason why

4. ASK in order to GET

As with all other steps, the more you practice and know these steps the easier they will be to use in your own presentations. The faster you learn and implement these steps, the more success you'll see.

STEP 6: OBJECTIONS

When a prospect doesn't say yes, they have some objection to your offer. Typically the objections will be around time or money. They don't have the time and they don't have the money. The truth is that people will buy it if they want it. They'll find the time and the money because emotion is stronger than logic. We can prove this by looking at the things people buy like jewelry, cars, and gadgets. Why would someone pay thousands of dollars for a Rolex? The answer and the reason is because they see value and because they want it. Their brain says no, and yet something compels them to make the purchase.

The more we prepare for objections the more success we will see. If we don't hear a yes after presenting our offer, that means that we just didn't do a good enough job at finding their pain in the previous steps.

If their answer is no, we simply go back to the third step and try to uncover more pain through open-ended questions. Then we move on to the fourth step in order to show that we understand their pain and then move back to the 5th step to offer another solution.

Next we repeat the steps in the fifth step and simply ask for the sale again. This time we might come up with another option or some sort of alternative that might appeal to them. Or, maybe we just ask them what they want to see and what would cause them to take action to move forward today.

STEP 7: BACK END

Once your prospect agrees and commits to doing business with you, there are five steps we go through on the backend of the sale and they are:

1. Offer an upsell or a downsell as additional buying options.

2. Fulfillment of what you promised you can do and/or customer service.

NEW RULES OF SUCCESS

3. Follow up and give thanks and gratitude to show we appreciate them.

4. Ask for referrals and start the lead-generation process.

5. Form joint ventures and partnerships with affiliates who will generate leads for you. In return you pay them a flat fee or a percentage of the sale.

NEXT STEP FOR YOUR SUCCESS

Following these "New Rules of Sales Success" will set you apart from 95% of your competition. Now that you have the strategy and the system, it's up to you to have the guts to take action and apply these *7 Steps to Massive Offline Profits.* When you do, you'll be on your way to seeing massive results and profits for you and your business.

238

About Preston

Preston Rahn is an author, speaker, and coach who is regularly sought out by other leaders for his advice on high level marketing and sales strategies that really work. Preston is known for his unique perspective, which comes from his background in graphic design, creating websites, marketing and sales. Preston has been in sales his whole life, and started his online career in 1998 when he built his first website.

Over the years Preston started, founded and partnered with many businesses and currently enjoys coaching, consulting and training professionals to improve their sales process so they can make more money and have a better life. He created his own Easy Sales Process that helps professionals connect emotionally with their prospects, so they can "significantly improve their conversion of prospects to become clients in a fast and easy way."

To learn more about Preston Rahn and "The New Rules of Sales Success," visit: EasySalesProcess.com
Or connect directly with Preston by visiting: LinkedIn.com/in/PrestonRahn

CHAPTER 24

THE NEW RULES OF MARKETING SUCCESS

BY GREG ROLLETT

Business is a funny thing. We all want to succeed. We all want to impact more people through our work, our passions and our skillsets. Yet many business owners simply do not know how to go about doing this. They do not know about how to go out and find new clients, to uncover their true needs and desires, and give them the thing that will improve their life.

I know that marketing is the driving force behind business and I am on a mission to help people see the power that marketing can have when you believe in a product or service. It is the difference between healing the world in your health practice and seeing an obese population walk right past your doors. It is the difference between seeing a retiree go back to work because they didn't correctly plan for retirement and seeing another couple enjoy an afternoon on the beach.

No matter what business you are in, today you need to incorporate these five rules into your marketing in order to drive sales, increase revenues and have the impact you desire by sharing your products and services with the world.

RULE #1: YOUR MARKETING MUST BE DIRECT RESPONSE MARKETING

In a world where social media and smart phones seem to rule the land, the smart marketers know that for every dollar, minute of time or resource you allocate to something, you need to get something back. And a few new Twitter followers aren't going to do it.

When you are marketing today, you need to understand the numbers. How much money and time are you putting into something and how much money and time are you getting back. That is my definition of direct response marketing.

According to the Wikipedia and the Direct Response Advertising Glossary, direct response marketing is: *"A type of marketing designed to generate an immediate response from consumers, where each consumer response (and purchase) can be measured, and attributed to individual advertisements."*

In your business this means that you need to put in place response mechanisms that can quantify your marketing efforts. And this is where many business owners often turn the other cheek, continuing to guess what is and what isn't working.

If you do not know how many calls the Yellow Pages brought you this year, how many new clients or patients that turned into, and how much revenue was derived from that medium, how can you make a logical case for or against using that media again to attract new clients or patients?

You simply cannot.

This means you need to be ruthless with your tracking. You need to know what types of results to expect when your promotions are going to launch.

For starters, you need to start by tracking incoming phone calls. This is a very simple place to start. To begin, you simply leverage an RCF (remote call forwarding) service, which issues you a set of phone numbers that will forward to your current office line.

You then place these different and trackable phone numbers in your marketing. One number goes on your website, another in a direct mail campaign, another in your Yellow Pages ad and another on your catalog.

This allows you to consistently look at which source is producing calls and leads into your business. Once you know these very basic numbers, you can start to assess, in a logical manner, how these marketing media are performing.

You should also look into online analytics as well, from Google Analytics to more advanced tracking, to see if your websites and email marketing campaigns are converting the way that they should.

Many business owners create an auto responder (an automatic set of email messages that are sent to a prospect once they fill out a contact form on your website), but many cannot tell if those series of messages are producing any new clients or patients.

This is a big problem today and is the reason why Rule #1 has been put into place.

RULE #2: YOUR MARKETING MUST BE PERSONALITY DRIVEN

There is a definitive rule that we live by here, and that is *"People Buy People."* Taking that to another level, the rule becomes, *"people buy from people that they know, like and trust."*

If I have never heard of you, seen your face or know what you do, how can you expect me to buy from you?

Answering the above question if the reason for rule #2.

By nature, humans love interaction. We were meant to interact. It's why we have friends and social circles. It's why there are water cooler conversations. It is why we spend the majority of our lives looking for or staying in love with a significant other. It's why we bring other human beings into the world, raise them and they start the cycle all over again.

Your marketing is no different. It needs to connect with other humans. It needs to connect with them both emotionally and logically. The best way to do that is to sell yourself. Your clients and customers are going to buy because of who you are, and not necessarily what you do.

Let's take a car salesman. Today we can all look online and find a car that (a) fits our budget, (b) is the right color and (c) has all the specs that we want. And we can do all of that without ever setting a foot into a dealership.

So when we do step into a dealership and start talking to a salesman, there is going to be a connection, good or bad, and that is going to influence whether we buy the car from this dealer or not. It's how we connect with the sales person. We already know that you have the car we want. We already know the details and if we can afford it or not. We just want a knowledgeable, respectful salesman to help us make the decision and make the process fun.

That is what your marketing needs to do. It needs to connect with them so they feel they can trust you when it's time to take out their credit card or sign on the dotted line.

To put this into practice you need to show your face! Put your photo on everything you send out into the world. From your direct mail letters to the envelopes they go in. Put your photo at the top of your newsletter and in the header of your website. Put it in your ads and landing pages and everywhere in between.

Then you need to tell your story. This is why people will connect with you. We relate to stories more than we relate to facts. It's why we know the origin story of Superman, Spiderman and Batman. We can all relate to the stories of struggle they went through before they became superheroes.

Every time you get on stage, lead a teleseminar or webinar, as well as on your website and in sales pieces, you need to share a bit of you and your story. People will remember that story more than they will remember the facts of what you are presenting. And today, getting their attention and having them remember anything about you is monumental towards getting them to commit to do business with you.

RULE #3: NEVER RELY ON THE POWER OF 1 (ONE)

As a former touring musician, I would always converse with other musicians about getting the "big break" that we all desired to get us out of the fast food, roach motels and onto MTV and the tour buses. These conversations routinely ended up with someone saying, "if I could just find the 1(one) guy that will discover us and put us on the map."

And guess what? There was never that 1(one) guy. Ever.

The same holds true for your business. You need many people, many promotions and many steps to keep your business going.

For top musicians today, they are rely on tour managers, booking agents, producers, directors, costume designers, radio promoters, backup dancers and long stretches of touring to allow their fans to hear their music and generate their income.

Your business is the same, even if you are wearing multiple hats, which we all do at some point! What I want you to concentrate on is the fact that we are all too reliant upon one marketing channel or one promotion in our business.

Let's say back in the 80's you were fax blasting your way to success. And now, new regulations shut you and your fax operation down. That was the harsh reality for many business owners. The same thing happened to telesales operators who were cold-calling their way to success before the "do-not-call" list was established.

Today, far too many businesses rely on Google traffic or SEO and are at the mercy of Google's algorithm changes or slaps to Adwords accounts. And let's not get started on stamp prices rising. It is causing some mailers to cut back or fall off completely. All of this just goes to show that you cannot rest of your laurels and have just one source of business.

Then once you get the leads and prospects coming into your business, you cannot rely on one message to close the sale. Remember that we need to get them to know, like and trust you…and that rarely happens on a first, blind date.

Rather it happens over time. Through multiple mailings, emails, packages and phone calls. Having this follow-up system is paramount to your success today. Having it automated and systematized is even more important. Adding elements of personality and tracking the process (the first two rules for marketing success) is what will allow your marketing to break through and give you a definitive advantage in your marketplace.

RULE #4: YOU MUST KNOW YOUR MARKET BETTER THAN YOUR FAVORITE TV CHARACTER

When I am consulting with clients about their marketing, the first question I always ask revolves around, "who is your ideal client or customer for this product or service?"

Many times the response comes back very generalized or vague:

This product is for anyone that owns a home.

This service is for any small business with 2 or more employees.

I help baby boomers within 5 years of retirement.

I hope that you can already see that having these types of responses makes it very difficult to create a definitive winning marketing strategy.

When I receive answers like this, I go right into an exercise that I want you to go through right now as well. I want you to take out a sheet of paper and draw a line from the top to the bottom, right at the center of the page.

On the top left hand side I want you to write down the name of your favorite TV character. For myself, I will use Homer Simpson.

Next I want you to write down 4-6 things that you know about that character:

- He is married to Marge.

- He has 3 kids, Bart, Maggie and Lisa.

- He works at the Nuclear Power Plant.

- His boss is Mr. Burns.

- Nis neighbor is Ned Flanders.

- He loves to drink Duff Beer at Moe's.

Now on the right hand side I want you to write the name of your ideal customer. For me, I will use Kevin Smith!

And then I want you to do the same exercise.

I bet this one is much tougher. Here is an example from my music marketing business:

- He is 18-27 years old.

- He works in the hospitality industry (restaurant or hotel due to the flex hours).

- He wears t-shirts with a corny slogan on it, a backwards hat, khaki shorts and flip-flops.

- He plays shows in dive bars and makes about $50.

- He plays 1/2 original songs and 1/2 cover songs.

- He longs for the day when he can quit that job and play music full-time.

Knowing what I know about Kevin Smith, do you think that I can market effectively to him? Can I write copy that attracts him and connects with him emotionally? Can I use my personality to get in his head and build a bond with him?

You bet! And once you do this exercise with your ideal client it will become clearer for you as well. And if you know more about your favorite TV star than your client, you are in big trouble.

RULE #5: SHOW UP LIKE THE BIG MAN ON CAMPUS

Today it's easy to get caught up in sending people a link. "Here's a link to our services page." "Here's a link to our new video, check it out and let us know if you have any questions."

It has become the norm and if everyone is doing it, no one is standing out. No one is getting the attention of the market. This is where you change the game.

I want you to think back to a party that you went to in high school or college and as you were having a conversation with someone, the door opened and in walked this character that made everyone stop what they were doing and pay attention. They were the show stopper. The talk of the party.

This is what you need to do with your marketing. The reason is that we are so busy in our daily lives that almost nothing makes us...STOP. How can you stop your prospect dead in their tracks and give you their undivided attention?

By showing up like the BMOC – Big Man On Campus!

When a prospect calls into your office for more information, don't send them a link, fire out a FedEx package with a DVD, a sales letter and a catalog that they can hold in their hands.

How many links do we get sent every day?

How many packages show up at our door?

And when that package shows up, what else are they doing? Nothing but looking at what you sent.

And it doesn't have to be FedEx, but it has to thump. It has to be something they hold in their hands. Something that pulls their attention away from their Inbox, from Facebook, from their kids, from their online browsing and shopping and from all the commotion that eats up our lives.

And it also must include the previous four rules ahead of it. There must be a CTA, a call-to-action with a tracking number so you can justify the shipping spend.

There must be personality infused within the package from a copy of your book, to a catalog with your picture on it, to a letter that goes through your origin story.

And then you will follow-up with them with another piece a few days later. Never relying on them to take action after the first gesture.

And then you will send items that match the needs, the emotions and the wants of the market because you know exactly what their hot buttons are.

When you put these five ingredients together, you will win.

You will get more business.

And you will create the lifestyle that you desire.

About Greg

Greg Rollett, the ProductPro, is a best-selling author and online marketing expert who works with authors, experts, entertainers, entrepreneurs and business owners from all over the world to help them share their knowledge and change the lives and businesses of others. After creating a successful string of his own educational products, Greg began helping others in the production and marketing of their own products.

Greg is a front-runner in utilizing the power of social media, direct response marketing and customer education to drive new leads and convert those leads into long-standing customers and advocates.

Previous clients include Coca-Cola, Miller Lite, Warner Bros and Cash Money Records, as well as hundreds of entrepreneurs and small-business owners. Greg's work has been featured on FOX News, ABC, and the Daily Buzz. Greg has written for Mashable, the Huffington Post, AOL, AMEX's Open Forum and more.

Greg loves to challenge the current business environments that constrain people to working 12-hour days during the best portions of their lives. By teaching them to leverage technology and the power of information, Greg loves helping others create freedom businesses that allow them to generate income, make the world a better place and live a radically ambitious lifestyle in the process.

A former touring musician, Greg is highly sought after as a speaker, having appeared on stages with former Florida Gov. Charlie Crist, best-selling authors Chris Brogan and Nick Nanton, as well as at events such as Affiliate Summit.

If you would like to learn more about Greg and how he can help your business, please contact him directly at: greg@productprosystems.com or by calling his office at: 877.897.4611.

You can also download a free report on how to create your own educational products at: www.productprosystems.com.